SEE
AUSTRALIA
AND
DIE

SEE AUSTRALIA AND DIE

Tales of misadventure down under

WENDY LEWIS

NEW
HOLLAND

First published in Australia in 2007 by
New Holland Publishers (Australia) Pty Ltd
Sydney • Auckland • London • Cape Town

1/66 Gibbes Street Chatswood NSW 2067 Australia
218 Lake Road Northcote Auckland New Zealand
86 Edgware Road London W2 2EA United Kingdom
80 McKenzie Street Cape Town 8001 South Africa

A record of this book is held at the National Library of Australia.

ISBN: 9781741105834

Publisher: Martin Ford
Project Editor: Lliane Clarke
Designer: Natasha Hayles
Production Assistant: Liz Malcolm
Printer: Ligare Book Printers, Sydney, New South Wales

10 9 8 7 6 5 4 3 2 ✦

For Ben

Timor
Sea
Finniss River •   ■ Darwin
                 KAKA
                 NATIONAL

INDIAN
OCEAN

•Prince Regent River

Broome ●

Great Sandy Desert

NORT
TERRI

KARIJINI
NATIONAL
PARK

WESTERN
AUSTRALIA

•Yulara
•Uluru

SC
AUS

•Laverton

■
Perth

Great Australian
Bight

SOUTHERN OCEAN

Torres Strait

Sea

Cape
York
Peninsula

Coral Sea

Julatten • • Port Douglas
• Cairns

Whitsunday Islands

Tully • • Hinchinbrook Is.

GREAT BARRIER REEF
MARINE PARK

Townsville •

• Hayman Is.
• Hamilton Is.

QUEENSLAND

PACIFIC
OCEAN

• Birdsville

gs

• Fraser Is.

IA

• Lake Eyre

Brisbane ■

• Moreton Is.
• North Stradboke Is.

• Bonalbo

NEW SOUTH
WALES

• Manilla

• Wisemans Ferry
■ Sydney
• Coledale

ACT

• Thredbo and Snowy Mountains

VICTORIA

• Eden

■ Adelaide

■ Melbourne

Tasman Sea

Bass Strait

TASMANIA

■ Hobart

Contents

8: BILLABONG

9: OUTBACK

10: SKY

REFERENCES

Introduction

This book is about dangerous Australia. It's about relentless heat; creatures that can kill in minutes; the cruelty of nature. The great majority of holidaymakers in Australia get home in one piece but a handful do suffer fatal or serious non-fatal injuries. These carefully researched stories give you the facts about real life-threatening situations that locals and overseas tourists have faced as they travel around Australia. Some are well-known, many are not. This book takes the raw elements of Australia—the ocean, the sky, the billabongs, the Outback—and shows how chilling they can be.

An alien land

For thousands of years, Aboriginal people have had a close relationship with the land. When Europeans arrived, they found a totally alien landscape. The animals were like nothing they had ever seen. Some, like the platypus, they could scarcely believe were real at all. The sun burnt their delicate white skin, the soil was useless and the bush was a place to fear.

The mythology of the bush is a strong part of the Australian psyche. In the early days of the colony, convicts would escape and 'go bush'. The ones that survived were the ones with the sense to join up with Aborigines who showed them how to find food. Young children wandered into the bush and were lost, sometimes forever. Artists like Frederick McCubbin captured the dream-like aura of the Australian bush with evocative works like *Lost* (1886). Joan Lindsay's novel-later-turned-film *Picnic at Hanging Rock* (1975) played exquisitely with the haunting qualities of the Australian bush in its story of four schoolgirls who go on a bush picnic and never return.

Some early explorers met with similar fates. The overly ambitious Ludwig Leichhardt set off in 1848 to cross the continent from east to west but his entire expedition was never heard from again. Burke and Will's famous attempt at a south-to-north crossing in 1860 was a disaster too. Burke's stubborn refusal to accept readily offered help from Aboriginal people led to them both starving to death. Time and time again, Australia shows itself to be a country that swallows up the unwary.

Some of the people in these pages are unwary. Gabriele Grossmueller who died alone in the burning sands of South Australia is a tragic example. There are adventurers who set out on great quests like the amazing, survival-savvy Robert Bogucki. There are those who die agonising deaths, victims of tiny invisible jellyfish, like Richard Jordan and Robert King. Some are tales of classic risk-takers, like our very own Steve Irwin. Some involve human error, like the story of the tour guide who gave the go-ahead for his group to swim in a billabong full of crocodiles. Many, like shark victim Sarah Whiley, are simply in the wrong place at the wrong time. Some are unprepared, ignorant or even foolish. But mostly they set out to enjoy themselves, experience new things and make the most of that strange thing we call life.

This book's structure is shaped by the elements of Australia: the beach, the bush, the mountains, to name but a few. Each section begins with data about the person/s involved in the story, followed by an account of what happened to them on that particular day. Some stories are followed by 'Did you Know …?' facts, with related information, bizarre coincidences or anecdotes. It's the kind of book you can read cover-to-cover or dip into at leisure, preferably while sitting on a sub-tropical island off the Queensland coast or waiting for the sun to set behind Uluru in the Red Centre. All in all, *See Australia and Die* is a fascinating insight into a wild and beautiful country.

PS: See Naples and *what* …?

For all you literati out there, you may have heard an old Italian saying, 'Vedi Napoli e poi muori', roughly translated as 'See Naples and die'. This expression was around at a time when Naples was a major European city, beaten only in opulence and population by London and Paris. It didn't mean that Naples was full of wild beasts that would make a meal out of any unwitting visitor. It meant that Naples was so exquisite, so sublime, that having seen its beauty one would be content to die. Australia is like that. If you have seen the Red Centre, the mighty Kimberley, the tangled rainforests of the Daintree; if you have seen the rocks, the rivers and the coral reefs, then you may well be content to die, feeling there is nothing left to see.

1.
Ocean

The Great Barrier Reef is another world: a world of bizarrely-shaped corals rising up like forests, sea turtles, giant clams with gaping mouths and millions of fish. In these stories, you can read about snorkellers on the reef; one who lives through an unprovoked shark attack, another who goes snorkelling and never comes back. There's the skipper who sees his two best friends taken by a shark right before his eyes; the trail of tragedy left by the tiny but deadly irukandji; and the story of the infamous black ray that ended the life of the much-loved and seemingly unstoppable Steve Irwin. But first up, the mystery of two divers left behind on an outer reef to die.

SCUBA DIVING

THE COUPLE LEFT BEHIND TO DIE

Name:	**Thomas Lonergan and Eileen Lonergan**
Age:	**33 years old and 28 years old**
Nationality:	**American**
Incident:	**Missing, presumed drowned**
When:	**26 January 1998**
Where:	**St Crispin Reef, off Port Douglas, Queensland**
Outcome:	**Fatal**

If there is a tourist disappearance that has had more than its fair share of conspiracy theories, it's this one. Thomas and Eileen Lonergan were left behind at the end of a day's dive on St Crispin Reef, off Port Douglas, in 1998. This in itself is utterly shocking, but the media frenzy and the theories tossed around to explain their disappearance ranged from quite reasonable to totally loopy. Were they picked up by a 'mystery boat'? Had they faked their disappearance? Were they abducted by the CIA?

As weeks rolled on, the theories became even more fantastic. Diary entries revealed that Thomas Lonergan had fantasised about doing away with himself. Various pieces of their diving gear were progressively washed ashore. A look-alike couple in a freshly spray-painted car was pursued by a news crew. The Lonergans' disappearance has all the ingredients of an overblown work of pure fiction, but it isn't. It's ultimately a story of great sadness unlikely to ever reach resolution. It will remain: a shattered dive company, grieving families and two lives forever lost.

Childhood sweethearts

Thomas and Eileen Lonergan worked as teachers with the US Peace Corps in Fiji and Tuvalu. They had adapted well to remote island life and after three years were looking forward to heading home via Australia, Indonesia, Thailand, India and then through Europe back to the US where they planned to settle down and have children. The manager of the hostel in Port Douglas where the Lonergans were staying remembered them as the smiling young Americans. They were childhood sweethearts who had married straight out of college. Inseparable, husband and wife, best friends.

Sunday 25 January was like any other day on the reef – blue sky, calm sea, crystal clear water with good visibility. The Lonergans left Port Douglas at 8.30am on the *MV Outer Edge* for a day's diving. The boat headed out past Snapper Island towards the magnificent coral reefs that make up the Great Barrier Reef.

On board, they were briefed on diving sites and safety procedures. As they arrived at each dive site, they were told the lie of the reef and given instructions for the dive. The Lonergans dived twice with other passengers in 20 metre deep water. They were told to go only to 12 metres and to remain down no longer than 40 minutes.

After lunch aboard the boat, the group of 26 was ready to make their final dive for the day. The Lonergans wanted to do their third dive alone. They were given permission and told to be back on board by 3pm.

3pm. Time to go. At 3.10pm, the skipper started the engines. Once the ladders were brought up and the transom closed, the boat waited another 10-15 minutes while the crew cleaned the gear on the back deck, overlooking the dive site. Karl—one of the crew—went down with snorkel, mask and fins to retrieve the anchor. He looked over the whole dive site but saw no bubbles, nobody, nothing to indicate there were divers still there.

Most dive boats use the same procedure: a blast on a whistle to get people out of the water, a head count to make sure everyone is on board, and then back to Port Douglas. But routines can be lax. Divers do dive without being recorded in any logbook. And headcounts can be wrong. If the number is less, there's a recount, if the number is more, it's assumed all is OK. It appears no specific attempt was made to confirm the Lonergans' return to the boat that day, even though they had been authorised to dive separately. The headcount that day got the right number but the wrong number of people were on the boat. Two were missing. And unbelievable as it seems, no one noticed until two days later.

The next day

It's now Tuesday morning, 27 January. *MV Outer Edge* went out as usual. The Lonergans' bags were still on board, but the crew assumed whoever owned them would be back to get them. But when they opened up one of the bags, a crew member was startled to find Thomas Lonergan's wallet.

On Tuesday night, they rang the Lonergans' hostel only to find that they hadn't been seen since leaving for the day on Sunday morning. That night Karl was celebrating his birthday at the Ironbar when he received a phone call. The Dive Operations Manager had just informed police that two divers were missing.

Wednesday 28 January. A search by 12 planes, three helicopters and a flotilla of boats failed to find any trace of the Lonergans. But how effective is a search commencing more than 60 hours after the missing persons were last seen? The next day the search was scaled down; the sobering conclusion was that the Lonergans' survival chances were virtually nil. The three-day search, estimated to cost $150, 000, extended about 88 nautical miles south of the reef, 74 nautical miles north and 35 nautical miles east. Despite 58 aerial sweeps, 17 fixed-wing aircraft and three helicopters, nothing was found. On Friday 30 January, the search was abandoned. Relatives in the USA were in shock. The Queensland Government offered a formal apology. And speculation, rumours and theories sprang up and kept on spreading.

Why didn't the couple swim to the pontoon? Conditions that afternoon were perfect. The sea was a warm 29°C, underwater visibility was good and there was virtually no current. *Wy Knot*, a beche de mer diving boat, was anchored less than six kilometres away while a game fishing boat was a similar distance away on the other side of the reef. The Quicksilver pontoon was also about six kilometres to the north. They could have swum west to a channel marker beacon or let the NW current take them to the sandbank on Mackay Reef. The Lonergans were confident and fit. They had at least four to five hours of daylight left. They had wetsuits and inflatable jackets and should have easily swam to the pontoons or reef or one of the boats nearby.

The media speculated when Queensland police suggested that personal items left behind by the Lonergans indicated trauma in their lives. Eileen Lonergan's diary revealed that her husband was depressed and felt he had nothing left to live for after giving three years of his life to the Peace Corps. He felt he had achieved all his goals and worried that it would be difficult to start a new life back in his old stamping ground. She also wrote that he talked often about dying and could not bear the thought of her living alone. But why go on an organised tour if you plan to kill yourself? Besides, the Lonergans had booked the rest of their trip home. They had filled out the guest register in their hostel, writing their next destination as Denpassar, Indonesia.

In San Diego, Eileen Lonergan's father, John Hains, said the family was not considering legal action against the dive company. He acknowledged the effort being put into the search and that the people who ran the charter would carry the burden for the rest of their lives: 'Their lives are going to be wrecked … my heart and prayers go out to them.'

On 3 February, a buoyancy vest was found on a remote beach 115 kilometres north of Cairns. But after checking a detailed list of the Lonergans' equipment, police concluded it wasn't theirs. Two days later, another vest was found at Indian Heads, about 10 kilometres north of Cooktown. This time the black and green Sea Pro vest had five crucial handwritten words: 'Tom Lonergan, Peace Corp, Fiji'. This raised hope that perhaps the Lonergans were alive. A six-member Special Emergency Response Team was called in because of the dangers of crocodiles and marine stingers.

Police said the vest was in good condition and showed no signs of damage. It was unbuckled. The sand covering it indicated it had been lying on the beach for less than 12 hours. Nothing in the pockets gave away any clues. A disposable camera found 500 metres away wasn't theirs. No traces of footprints were found anywhere near the scene.

On 8 February, police found a flipper and an underwater camera believed to be the Lonergans', but the film had no exposures. Three days later, Eileen's wetsuit hood was found. A dive tank was found the next day; and on 15 February, Hopevale Aboriginal Community gave police a second dive tank they'd found on the beach near Indian Heads. The search was agonising. Dive tanks, buoyancy vests ... but no trace of the Lonergans.

Conspiracy theories

Many theories sprang up to explain the couple's disappearance. On the day the Lonergans disappeared, there were three boats in the vicinity of St Crispin Reef. Two were accounted for, one was dubbed the 'mystery boat'. This was tied in with the discovery of alleged links between the Lonergans and another American, Milton Windsor Harris, who faked his disappearance from a New Zealand ferry in 1985 and took out life insurance policies worth over $4 million before he was discovered living in Auckland four years later. The weird thing was that this man was from Baton Rouge in Louisiana, a member of the First Uniting Methodist Church and a member of the US Peace Corps. Just like the Lonergans.

Then, there was the mystery of the 'look-alike couple'. In late February, police spotted a couple stopping for petrol about four kilometres out of Cooktown. Their Landcruiser looked as if it had been painted blue in a rush paint job. They were approached by a TV camera crew but seemed anxious to leave. They said they were heading north, but they drove south. The TV crew tailed them but didn't catch up with them for 30 kilometres. When asked if they were the Lonergans, they laughed and the man asked if there was a reward for finding them. The man, who appeared to have a faint American accent, showed a remarkable likeness to Thomas Lonergan, except that he had more hair. When asked where they came from, the man hesitated and then said Spain. Police checked out the story but were unconvinced of any Lonergan connection.

A dive operator who took an all-Italian group to the reef the day after the Lonergans disappeared told police that the headcount on the return journey was three more than on the trip out to the reef. And he distinctly thinks he heard American accents. Later, at the trial, nine witnesses would be called to tell the jury of possible sightings of the pair in the days after their disappearance.

The most likely explanation was the simplest. The Lonergans had drowned. It was extremely hot that day and the N–NW winds late in the afternoon would have pushed anyone out to sea. The Lonergans would have been tired and dehydrated. It's all very well to say they could have simply swum to a pontoon, but it would have been separated from them by a deep channel with a strong current. To try and swim across the channel would have been highly risky. And being on the northern tip of St Crispin, they may not have even been able to see it. It seems they did what divers are supposed to do in such circumstances: they ditched weights and tanks and took off their vests to make swimming easier.

In late June, a diving slate (the writing board used by divers to communicate underwater) was found in mangroves at Archers Point, about 20 kilometres south of Cooktown and 170 kilometres north of Cairns. It had the Lonergans' names, address and US phone number. And it was dated 8am 26 January, the morning after they were left behind. Police confirmed that, in part, it read: 'please help us' and 'rescue us'. Was it a hoax? Members of the dive industry believed so, but police were inclined to believe it was real. Those who thought it was fake had some points in their favour. For a start, most diving slates sink, so how was it washed up on the shore? Second, it was most unusual for divers to write nearly a foolscap page-full of notes in small, neat handwriting. And thirdly, the fact that it had showed up just before the preliminary inquest was a little too coincidental.

The inquest

The wheels of the law were turning. A *prima facie* case existed against the dive boat company and its management; prosecution would follow. And it did. The inquest began in July. The findings would vindicate the couple's families—particularly the Lonergan family—who grew tired of the rumours springing up around them. Thomas' mother, Elizabeth, pointed out that there were too many people all too keen to find some outlandish reason why they weren't on the boat that afternoon. As she succinctly put it, they were left behind and that was the end of the story.

Coroner Noel Nunan found that theories of murder-suicide and faked disappearance were far-fetched. Their diaries showed the Lonergans were young, idealistic and in love. Tom was at a crossroads in his career, he had a restless nature and occasional dark thoughts; but they were interested in religion, art, nature and beauty. On 10 October 1998, Coroner Nunan found that Thomas and Eileen Lonergan had died at sea from drowning, exposure or shark attack some time between 8am on 26 January 1998 and 2 February 1998.

He committed Geoffrey Ian 'Jack' Nairn, the 43-year-old skipper, to stand trial for manslaughter. Nairn pleaded not guilty to criminal negligence causing the deaths of Thomas and Eileen Lonergan and, after less than 90 minutes, the Supreme Court jury agreed with him. Jack Nairn's parents reacted with tears; Jack himself made no immediate comment. And then Eileen Lonergan's parents displayed the forgiveness they had already shown. Elaine's mother hugged him; Elaine's dad embraced him too and whispered that it was OK.

Did you know?

Two American women died in separate water-related tragedies within 24 hours of each other in Queensland in May 2003: one at Agincourt Reef, off Port Douglas; the other in Mossman. On 30 May, 23-year-old Maren Dell was on a day trip with her brother, doing a resort dive. She was several metres underwater with an instructor when she got into difficulties clearing her mask. Next thing, she had a panic attack. The instructor took her to the surface but, in her agitated state, she surfaced too quickly and lost consciousness. Possibly she held her breath as she ascended, producing a serious condition called embolism, similar to the bends. She died from a massive heart attack. In a macabre coincidence, a 20-year-old American student drowned the next day on 31 May while swimming in a flooded waterhole. A group of students from Illinois Westland University were in Australia taking part in a marine biology course, visiting Mossman Gorge National Park. The young woman got dragged under a rock by a strong current and her friends couldn't pull her free. Her body was recovered by Navy rescue divers.

SHARK

Sharks set off a hard-wired primal response in most people. And that response is fear. If we encounter them, we are in their territory not our own, and they have a definite advantage. Australia has 175 species of shark, roughly half the world's total. Some are aggressive by nature—bull sharks, dusky whalers, great whites and tiger sharks among them—but the majority of Australian sharks are rather more placid and unlikely to attack; grey nurses, wobbegongs and leopard sharks, for example. More people have been killed by sharks in Australian waters than anywhere else in the world, but that adds up to less than 200 shark fatalities in the last 200 or so years. All in all, the chance of being attacked by a shark is remote. But then again, statistically improbable events do happen.

THE SHARK THAT ATE MY MATES

Name:	**Ray Boundy**
Age:	**28 years old**
Nationality:	**Australian**
Incident:	**Shark attack**
When:	**25 July 1983**
Where:	**Broadhurst Reef, off Townsville, Queensland**
Outcome:	**Non-fatal**

Name:	**Dennis Murphy**
Age:	**24 years old**
Nationality:	**Australian**
Incident:	**Shark attack**
When:	**25 July 1983**
Where:	**Broadhurst Reef, off Townsville, Queensland**
Outcome:	**Fatal**

Name:	**Lindy Horton**
Age:	**21 years old**
Nationality:	**Australian**
Incident:	**Shark attack**
When:	**25 July 1983**
Where:	**Broadhurst Reef, off Townsville, Queensland**
Outcome:	**Fatal**

The headlines tell it all: 'Skipper's ordeal: shark ate two friends' was the front page of *The Sydney Morning Herald* on 27 July 1983. 'Girl eaten by shark' screamed the afternoon paper, *The Daily Mirror*, on the same day. The sobering thing is that the headlines were true. This is the story of a fishing trip gone wrong, true friendship and the ultimate sacrifice.

Three friends set out

A 14 metre trawler, *New Venture* left Townsville Harbour on Sunday 24 July 1983. On board were three crew members who were also best mates. There was the skipper, 28-year-old Ray Boundy; the deckhand Dennis Murphy, 24, known as Smurf, and Smurf's girlfriend, Lindy Horton, the cook.

This was only Lindy's second time as a ship's cook. She had left an office job a couple of weeks before to try something more adventurous. On that Sunday, however, the wind was howling and she didn't want to leave port. But the realities of commercial fishing are brutal. It's a cutthroat industry and the costs of running a trawler are high. Bills keep coming in, insurance premiums skyrocket and fishing vessels do go out in less than perfect conditions …

Sunday night was when they ran into difficulties. The vessel was trawling near Broadhurst Reef, about 90 kilometres from Townsville, when a boom broke. The two men were busy securing the boom when a giant wave smashed against the trawler. It capsized.

The trio propped themselves up on the upturned hull. They got hold of a surfboard, a lifebuoy and three large pieces of foam and tied them together with fishing line. This would be their makeshift life raft.

At about 1am Monday, the three friends found themselves adrift on the vast expanse of ocean. They paddled and drifted all that day. They made light of what many would find terrifying. They laughed and joked, telling each other they were going to make it. The SE breeze was blowing them towards Keeper and Lodestone Reefs where they knew there would be other boats working. They would be OK.

Shark sighted

Nightfall. 7.30pm. A shark started to follow them. Ray was familiar with sharks and wasn't unduly worried. He reckoned it was a tiger shark, about four metres long. It started circling them. Then it swam right up to the float and started nudging it. But it was just too much when it lunged at his foot.

Ray kicked it off with his other foot and the shark retreated. He joked with Smurf that they weren't ready to be the shark's dinner just yet. Five minutes later, a big wave knocked the three of them into the water. The shark made its move. It went straight for Dennis. 'He's got my leg! The bastard's got my leg!' he screamed. Ray yelled out to kick at it as hard as he could, but it was too late.

The shark pulled Dennis under a couple of times. He surfaced. And then he gasped his final words: 'Well, it looks like that's it. You and Lindy bolt because he'll be back for the rest of me.'

With that, Dennis Murphy turned and swam straight for the shark. He managed four strokes. As Ray and Lindy began frantically paddling in the opposite direction they heard his final screams. Ray turned to see the shark lift his mate out of the water and thrust him head first into its jaws.

Lindy was hysterical. Ray had to slap her to get her to calm down. Earlier that evening, they had been laughing and joking but now all they could do was drift on in silence in their makeshift lifeboat of foam. With each minute they were getting closer to the safety of the reef. But with each minute, that unspoken fear was magnified. And what they dreaded the most finally happened. At 4am, the shark came back.

Lindy was sitting in the sling of the lifebuoy with her feet up on the foam. Ray was holding her hand, trying to keep her spirits up. When he saw the shark he felt pretty certain that it was the same one.

This time, the shark swam very slowly alongside them. Then, in one sudden motion, it reared out of the water and grabbed Lindy's upper body, shaking her like a rag doll. One squeal pierced the air and then, nothing. Ray believes it happened so fast, Lindy wouldn't have realised what was happening.

Ray had to get away. With only two pieces of foam to cling to, he paddled as fast as he could towards the reef. But he was followed by the shark. It tracked him for hours, circling in ever tightening circles.

'I had lost the two best friends I ever had and now he had come back for me,' he remembers thinking (*The Sydney Morning Herald*, p. 1, 27 July 1983). He didn't know it, but every boat in the Townsville trawling fleet was out looking for him over a 130,000 square kilometre search area. And a coastal search plane was nearing.

At daybreak, he spotted the breakers of Lodestone Reef. And he saw the rescue plane overheard. That's when he knew that the shark was not going to get him.

The final swim for freedom

Ray knew that if he could make it to the outer reef, the shark wouldn't follow. But it was right behind him. Then a wave came, a life-saving wave. Ray caught it onto the outer reef. He remembers yelling out triumphantly to the sea: 'You won't get me now!' (ibid).

He had made it after 36 hours in the water. He had paddled and floated about 60 kilometres. He struggled to shore, laughing at the madness of it all. He had lacerations to his arms from the coral, he had seen unimaginable horror, but he was on dry land. The magnitude of the ordeal suddenly hit him. He sank to the ground and sobbed.

THE HAMMERHEAD THAT LUNGED AT LIENNE

Name:	**Lienne Schellekens**
Age:	**18 years old**
Nationality:	**Dutch**
Incident:	**Shark attack**
When:	**29 December 2002**
Where:	**Upolu Cay, near Cairns, Queensland**
Outcome:	**Non-fatal**

When a hammerhead attacked an 18-year-old Dutch tourist near Cairns in 2002, locals were quick to say what an unusual event it was. The helicopter pilot who air-lifted her to Cairns Airbase Hospital couldn't remember the last shark bite in the area. Others recalled the last attack was 15 years earlier at Opal Reef, 75 kilometres north of Cairns. That time, a German tourist and an Australian had each been bitten on the arm by a hammerhead. The striking thing about shark attacks is how rare they are.

The diving expedition

Travelling solo after finishing high school, Lienne Schellekens came all the way from the Netherlands to see some of the millions of fish and thousands of individual coral reefs that make up the Great Barrier Reef.

She was part of a group that left Cairns on the catamaran *Daytripper* at about 8.30am on Sunday 29 December 2002. The skipper, Chris Adams, and his wife Frances had been running dive expeditions in the area for three years. The group of 27 headed for Upolu Cay, a popular diving area about 40 kilometres NE of Cairns. Tour boats and dive boats are a familiar sight here. Aggressive sharks are not.

It was about 2.30pm and Lienne was in the water with three other snorkellers. She didn't see the shark until it was two metres away. From her description, it was probably a hammerhead. It was big—its head spanned about 0.5 metres across—and it was travelling very fast when she got the shock of her life. It was coming straight at her.

In a totally unprovoked attack, the hammerhead grabbed Lienne's left arm. She screamed as it ripped chunks of flesh off. Chris Adams, the skipper, heard her screaming and, without knowing what was happening, jumped into his dinghy. As he came closer, the water began to turn red with blood and the horrible realisation struck him: a shark attack. Despite the danger, the snorkellers in the group stuck with the terrified teen. Chris later praised their bravery.

The rescue

Luckily, after its vicious initial lunge, the shark seemed to lose interest. So Chris was able to drag Lienne from the water, into the dinghy and back onto the boat. She was conscious but her left arm was severely savaged with deep lacerations to the forearm and upper arm. Chris had to think fast. A group of divers had just gone down for half an hour. The catamaran's rescue boat was keeping an eye on them and they couldn't be left unattended. He couldn't get her to Upolu Cay by himself; he needed to contact another reef cruiser for help.

Another dive boat, *Ocean Spirit II*, was nearby and responded to the emergency call within minutes. The skipper, *Ocean Spirit II* crew and paramedics did what they could to stem the bleeding and took Lienne to Upolu Cay, about two kilometres away, to wait for the Queensland Rescue helicopter. It was now about an hour after the shark attack and Lienne's condition was stable. The helicopter pilot thought she'd survive but that she'd need a fair few stitches.

Lienne was airlifted to Cairns Base Hospital where the pilot's assessment proved correct. Fortunately, her arm was not severed but she did need surgery immediately. She spent the first week of the new year in hospital recovering from her ordeal. As news spread, she got lots of visitors including fellow Dutch tourists who happened to be in Cairns at the time.

One week after the attack, Lienne boarded a flight for the Netherlands, leaving the coral reefs far behind. She was still in a weakened state and would need ongoing long-term muscle reconstruction to heal her wounds. But she was glad to be going home.

Did you know?

Macabre but true, another young Dutch tourist made headlines in Far North Queensland less than two weeks after Lienne Schellekens' shark attack. Jan-Paul Swagemakers, 25 years old, died while snorkelling at Saxon Reef off Cairns on 9 January 2003. Conditions were calm, the water was shallow and he was part of a supervised group dive. So what went wrong? Possibly 'shallow water blackout' which can occur when a confident diver stays underwater too long, attempts to surface and runs out of oxygen. The scuba instructor found him unconscious, his body draped over some coral. He immediately surfaced with the body and began resuscitation while the dive boat sailed three kilometres to a pontoon to meet the Queensland Rescue helicopter. But by the time the helicopter arrived, Jan-Paul was dead.

IRUKANDJI

I rukandji commonly refers to one species of jellyfish—*carukia barnesi*—but these days it's believed there may be up to 10 different species that cause the excruciating condition known as 'irukandji syndrome'. The irukandji is a tiny translucent jellyfish, virtually invisible in the water. It's found off the northern coast of Australia from Broome in Western Australia to Rockhampton, Queensland. It is a relative of the larger lethal box jellyfish—*chironex fleckeri*—which has caused 71 fatalities since 1884, predominantly among young Australian children who die within minutes of being stung.

The irukandji is much rarer and much less is known about it. What is known is that when it brushes against something—say a hapless swimmer—it releases millions of microscopic harpoons that shoot tiny barbed venom-filled needles into the victim's skin. Then follows skyrocketing blood pressure, pounding heart rate, sweating, nausea, stress hormones flooding the body, agony, brain haemorrhaging and death. There is no known anti-venom.

TWO MEN AND THE TINY INVISIBLE KILLER

Name:	**Richard Jordan**
Age:	**58 years old**
Nationality:	**British**
Incident:	**Irukandji**
When:	**31 January 2002**
Where:	**Hamilton Island, Queensland**
Outcome:	**Fatal**

Name:	**Robert King**
Age:	**44 years old**
Nationality:	**American**
Incident:	**Irukandji**
When:	**16 April 2002**
Where:	**Opal Reef, off Port Douglas, Queensland**
Outcome:	**Fatal**

Up Cairns way in Far North Queensland, the Irukandji people of Palm Cove have long known of the terrible sickness a certain jellyfish brings during the rainy season, roughly from November to May. But it wasn't until 2002 that the irukandji jellyfish made headlines by causing two fatalities within eleven weeks. Richard Jordan, a British tourist swimming in the warm shallows of the reef, was the first recorded irukandji fatality. Robert King, an American snorkelling off Port Douglas, would soon follow as the second.

Two men on holiday

Early in 2002, two men arrived in Australia on holidays. They never knew each other, they stayed in different resorts. But within eleven weeks they would both die in excruciating pain from the same cause. Richard Jordan was from Driffield in Yorkshire, UK, the Director of a property management firm and interior design company. Now that he was semi-retired with three adult children, Richard and his wife, Jean, were having some much-deserved time out. They were halfway through a two month round-the-world trip when they got to Hamilton Island, one of the resort islands on the Great Barrier Reef.

   Robert King was from Columbus, Ohio, in the USA. He was a research scientist for Nestlé; among his claims to fame was the invention of a new kind of machine for making ice cream cones. He was also fit, adventurous and had travelled widely. Before he'd set off on his eight-week holiday/ business trip to Australia, he'd discussed deadly native wildlife with his girlfriend, Michelle. But more likely than not, he was unaware of the real dangers of the irukandji.

A plague of jellyfish

The summer of 2002 saw a record high number of jellyfish in the tropical waters of northern Australia. Strong winds and abnormal wind patterns blew them towards shore and they were right at home in the unusually warm waters. Normally roughly 30 people are hospitalised with irukandji syndrome between November and May every year. But over December/January 2002, more than 80 people were treated for stings at Cairns Base Hospital alone. Netting on some beaches can keep box jelly fish out but not their much smaller relative. More jellyfish close to shore means a greater risk of rare and deadly subspecies coming into contact with humans for the first time.

At Hamilton Island Resort where the Jordans were staying, guests were warned about irukandji and advised to swim in the hotel pools rather than in the ocean. But the crystal clear waters were just too inviting. On Wednesday 30 January, Richard went for a swim in the warm shallows. He may have felt a slight pinprick or nothing at all as the tentacles of the translucent jellyfish brushed against him. He wouldn't have been aware that he had been stung. Even in the clearest waters, they are virtually impossible to detect.

For the first half hour, he felt nothing. But then came the onset of terrible pain: cramps, back ache and nausea. Jean Jordan took her husband to Hamilton Island Medical Centre where he collapsed and fell into a coma.

Richard was transported to Mackay Base Hospital on the mainland. He was put on a saline drip. Little is known about the toxin of the irukandji because they are so rare, but what is known is that the level of pain is excruciating. And it comes in waves of agony. Since there is no known antidote, the only treatment is massive doses of painkiller, equivalent to that given to someone in a near-fatal car crash. But it's not even certain that huge amounts of morphine can ease the pain.

Richard had gone through open-heart surgery in 1983. It's likely that the toxin aggravated his pre-existing heart and blood pressure conditions. And this brought on cerebral haemorrhaging. Richard Jordan died late on Thursday 31 January, having never regained consciousness.

Ten weeks later

On the Easter weekend in April 2002, Robert King was enjoying a spot of snorkelling off Opal Reef, Port Douglas. But when he climbed back on the boat to return to the mainland, he knew something was wrong. He rubbed his chest and uttered the portentous words, 'I don't feel so good.'

Robert King may have felt a slight stinging sensation, like sea lice crawling over the skin. But much worse was to come. And his descent into unconsciousness came rapidly.

By the time the emergency helicopter arrived, he was screaming in agony. He was airlifted to Townsville Hospital. A few hours later he was in a coma. Like Richard Jordan, a rapid rise in heart rate and skyrocketing blood pressure led to brain haemorrhaging, brain damage and death. Robert King died on 16 April, never having regained consciousness.

The deaths of these two men suggest that there may well have been earlier irukandji deaths, with the cause of death wrongly attributed to something else like heart attack or divers' decompression sickness. Robert King's family generously donated his heart to researchers to further existing knowledge of the irukandji. His organs were donated to Australians awaiting transplants. In this way, something positive sprang from his death.

Did you know?

Magnesium is a relatively new treatment for irukandji syndrome. And one man who owes his life to it is Chris Newbrook from Cardiff, Wales. He had a truly unforgettable honeymoon: spending two days of it in Intensive Care fighting for his life. It was December 2006 and Chris and Katherine were about halfway through a six-month round-the-world honeymoon. Chris was snorkelling near Hayman Island when he suddenly felt terrible pain shoot through his neck as if it was burning. He had chest pains, he couldn't breathe and he couldn't stop shaking.

He was airlifted to the Intensive Care Unit at Mackay Base Hospital and given magnesium to combat the release of stress hormones into the bloodstream. Magnesium works by reducing the effect of the rush of adrenalin and noradrenalin, shutting off the body's automatic response and thus lessening the risk of heart failure. The treatment worked. And Chris reckons he owes his life to it. After two days in Intensive Care, he was given the all clear. He hopped on a bus to Airlie Beach, on holiday once again. He and Katherine decided to continue touring the Whitsunday Islands before heading north to Cairns to do more snorkelling, of course. After all, he figured, what were the chances of being stung again?

SNORKELLING

THE WOMAN WHO NEVER CAME BACK

Name:	**Ursula Clutton**
Age:	**80 years old**
Nationality:	**American**
Incident:	**Missing, presumed drowned**
When:	**11 January 2000**
Where:	**Agincourt Reef, off Port Douglas, Queensland**
Outcome:	**Fatal**

After the Lonergans' still unsolved disappearance, the dive industry in Queensland was in for a considerable shake-up. Out of reviews of codes of practice, investigations and much hand-wringing came a list of recommendations. One was for dive operators to appoint a lookout to watch over dive areas. Another was to make safety logs for divers compulsory. Medical checks on divers and snorkellers was tossed around. Another recommendation was for a compulsory headcount and recount to be carried out by two staff members, so that the horror of being left behind on a dive would never happen again. A number of these recommendations became legislation in Queensland on 1 February 2000. Even so, it still didn't save the life of one American tourist.

Happy New Year

It's the start of the year 2000. The Y2K bug hasn't disabled world-wide communications and Armageddon hasn't come. Life goes on and it is pretty much business as usual. In Far North Queensland it was more of the same: hot summer days, high humidity and snorkelling in the magical underwater world of the Great Barrier Reef.

One Sunday in mid-January, US tourist Ursula Clutton arrived in Australia as part of a tour group starting a three-month holiday. Two days later, she went snorkelling at Agincourt Reef, just north of where Thomas and Eileen Lonergan had vanished two years earlier. Nervous members of the dive industry say there are no similarities between the two cases. It's true Ursula Clutton wasn't diving, she was snorkelling. And she certainly wasn't left behind: the dive company realised she was missing as soon as they did a headcount and recount. The eerie thing is that despite these technicalities, she too disappeared.

Ursula Clutton was a Down's syndrome therapist from Fort Bragg, California who loved travelling, adventure and the great outdoors. She'd climbed mountains, crossed rivers and had dreamed about coming to Australia for years. She was extremely fit and strong, a good swimmer and an experienced snorkeller. Ursula Clutton was also 80 years old, which makes her passions even more impressive. She was an amazing grey-haired powerhouse and she certainly wasn't going to slow down on her trip Down Under.

On the morning of 11 January, Ursula Clutton was up bright and early, looking forward to the day ahead. She and her friend Hollie Hollingsworth were going to Agincourt Reef, 50 kilometres NE of Port Douglas, and it was sure to be spectacular. It was a big group that went out that morning, about 315 all up. The dive company running the tour had been around for over 20 years and had taken more than two million tourists out to the reef in that time.

About 50 from the group went snorkelling that day, Ursula among them. All in all, the set-up was about as safe as it could be: the company seems to have acted on the post-Lonergan dive industry recommendations. There were safety lines marking out a clearly delineated snorkelling area. There was a lookout on watch at all times whose sole duty was to keep an eye on the snorkellers. There were safety staff on the snorkelling platform and there were semi-submersibles in the water, ready to pick up any snorkeller who started drifting away.

Missing

Ursula chose a spot very close to the pontoon—a safe place to be—but she was swimming alone. Hollie, who stayed on board, last saw her friend just after midday. Three hours later, when everyone boarded the catamaran to return to Port Douglas, an official headcount was carried out. There was one person missing. A recount got the same result.

In the wake of the Lonergan fiasco, the dive company was quick to point out that they did everything by the book. All snorkellers, Ursula Clutton included, were wearing life jackets. As required, a lookout was on duty but there had been no signs of anything amiss. And immediately prior to the catamaran leaving, two headcounts were carried out as recommended.

Later the company was a little defensive, trying to deflect any suggestion of wrongdoing on their part by pointing out that Ursula's friends hadn't informed them she wasn't on board until the last minute. Which is a fair point, but with such a large number of people onboard, it's reasonable for those in her group to assume that she was sitting or chatting with someone else at the other end of the boat. But this was no time to point the finger. Ursula Clutton was missing and the crew had to act fast.

The skipper immediately got hold of the one solitary unclaimed bag and rummaged through it to find some form of ID. The crew promptly started a search of the immediate area, radioed for another boat to come, called for a helicopter and notified police. Then, having done as much as they could, the catamaran set off on the return trip to Port Douglas with their 315 minus one passengers.

The search

The search failed to find any trace of Ursula Clutton. A massive air and sea search continued the next day with five aircraft and helicopters, navy divers and police boats covering over 625 square nautical miles. It continued the next day but it was now 48 hours since she had been reported missing. Hollie had been hoping for the best, knowing her friend's fighting spirit.

She believed that, with a lifejacket, Ursula would have had the strength to keep going. But her hopes faded when police discovered she must have removed her lifejacket.

Police called off the search for Ursula Clutton on 14 January. The belief in dive industry circles was that the cause of death was medical. She may have had a heart attack or stroke, in which case her body would have sunk to the bottom of the sea before being swept away by ocean currents.

Did you know?

While the aerial search for Ursula Clutton was going on, a second drama was unfolding right under their rotor blades. Two men spent a horrible night adrift in the water somewhere out near Opal Reef, about ten kilometres from the pontoon where Ursula Clutton went missing. At 3pm on 13 January 2000, two divers went out scuba diving for Crown of Thorn starfish and then did some snorkelling. Later they swam back to their six metre aluminium boat. The only trouble was, the boat wasn't there.

While they had been away, the anchor rope had snapped and the boat had drifted off to latitudes unknown. There aren't many options out there on the reef when you are boatless, except to stay awake and keep floating. The next day, in the early morning light, one of the men saw a boat in the distance and swam towards it. Happily, the skipper saw him and a dive instructor on board swam out to the rescue. Exhausted and with noticeably bloodshot eyes, the man was remarkably well, considering. The first thing he said was: 'My mate's still out there. We need to get a boat out and start looking for him.' The skipper radioed a helicopter overhead—the helicopter that happened to be searching for Ursula Clutton—and the man's mate was quickly found about one kilometre away.

STINGRAY

Smooth stingray, blue spotted ray, eagle ray … No matter what the variety of ray found in Australian waters, as of 2006 they will be indelibly linked with the death of Steve Irwin. Stingrays are found in the tropical waters of the Great Barrier Reef, in warm shallows and muddy swamps. They have been known to defend themselves by lashing out with their barbed whip-like tails, but a lot of the time their defence is to lie flat on the bottom of the ocean or swamp or mud flat, making them difficult to spot. To avoid stepping on them, the trick is to shuffle your feet as you walk along, which will make them effortlessly glide away.

Fatal stingray attacks in Australia are few and far between: there have been only three such deaths recorded in Australia although the first is not strictly official. The first known fatality was a man in Melbourne in 1945; the second a 12-year-old boy in Innisfail, Queensland in 1988—which you can read about below—and the third, the Crocodile Hunter himself.

STEVE IRWIN MEETS HIS MATCH

Name:	**Steve Irwin**
Age:	**44 years old**
Nationality:	**Australian**
Incident:	**Stingray**
When:	**4 September 2006**
Where:	**Batt Reef off Port Douglas, Queensland**
Outcome:	**Fatal**

'Andrew Denton: Animals don't scare you, but people do?
Steve Irwin: Fair dinkum, they do.'
(Television interview on *Enough Rope*, 6 October 2003)

When people die before their time, there is shock and disbelief. When the figure has an incredible international following, the shock is magnified many times. Steve Irwin was larger-than-life. He was an animal-crazy risk-taker, a larrikin, the boy from Essendon who never grew up. He lived on adrenalin and his life was devoted to filming, saving and educating people about wild animals: crocodiles, Bengal tigers, you name it. It's only natural that underlying every camera-framed stunt was the small, quiet thought that he may die prematurely and in tragic circumstances. So in one sense, his death was not unexpected. But in another sense, it was totally shocking. That's what's so confusing about Steve Irwin's life cut short: the mixed emotions that come from knowing it could happen any time, mingled with utter disbelief that it did happen.

Invincible and unstoppable

Steve Irwin wasn't one to sit down with a nice cup of tea and flick through the Sunday papers. He was out there, full-on, barging headlong into insanely perilous situations because he loved it. For many Australians he was a bit too larger-than-life, but millions of Americans lapped him up. Australians may not realise just how popular he was in the USA: he needed bodyguards and helicopter dummies to avoid crowds of adoring fans. On one US tour he appeared on *Jay Leno*, *Larry King Live* and *The Oprah Winfrey Show* and tirelessly did close to one thousand interviews; he even popped up in an episode of *South Park*, the mark of a true postmodern hero.

He polarised people. There were those who thought he was a fantastic ambassador for Australia and a passionate advocate for wildlife both in Australia and throughout the world. Then there were those who thought he was an embarrassing ocker who did stupid things. Like the time in January 2004 when he dangled his one-month-old baby boy a metre in front of a crocodile, supposedly to get little Bob used to the critters. It didn't go down well, with uncomplimentary comparisons to Michael 'Wacko' Jackson hanging his little baby, Paris, out a German window in 2002.

When you cut through all the hype and sensational news stories, it's pretty obvious that Steve Irwin was 'true blue'. He was genuine about the loves of his life: his mum and dad, his family and the animals of Planet Earth. He was not interested in the corporate world; a case in point is when he declined an invitation to dinner with Bill Clinton because it wasn't his thing. He was astonishingly generous with his time and with his money. True, he made millions and millions of dollars but he diverted the bulk of it back into animal conservation and animal welfare projects.

Another indisputable reality about Steve Irwin is that he constantly flirted with danger. That's what made him what he was. Once in Africa he crawled up to a pride of lions, never having worked with lions in his life. Much to the amazement of the camera crew, he got down on all fours and crawled right up to them, stood up, shouted, 'hey!' and they all ran off. That's fearlessness. Another time, he got a nasty bite from a two-metre Perenti lizard during a stage show in Alice Springs. He also had a near miss with two giant Komodo dragons which struck at him, going for his calf muscles with teeth like razors. He admitted afterwards that he had no idea of the danger he was getting himself into; the smell of blood could have sent the other dragons into a feeding frenzy.

In early 2006, he entertained a crowd of more than a thousand at the University of California by wrestling a rather large anaconda. Various news reports also breathlessly talked of him wrangling a Sumatran Tiger, orangutan, alligator, cobra, rattlesnake and more, all in the name of a 'G'day LA' promotion for Australia. Of course, his crocodile wrestling was the stuff of legends. DVDs like *Steve's Scariest Moments* (Volumes I and II), *Deadly Snakes* and *A Crocodile's Revenge* were all part and parcel of Steve Irwin and his unique way with animals.

The day before he died, Steve Irwin went swimming with a venomous two-metre sea snake. He stood in the chest-deep water, lifted the snake out and turned to the cameras: 'Here is the biggest sea snake I've ever seen in my life.' He explained to camera that even though the fangs were 'chockablock' full of venom, sea snakes were gentle creatures that only got aggro when they got angry. With that, the snake turned on him, causing Steve to exclaim,

'Lucky he didn't have his mouth open there. You could see how ol' Steve-o could've taken a hit!'

The day he died

The day Steve Irwin died, he was shooting a documentary with Philippe Cousteau, grandson of oceanographer extraordinaire, Jacques. Steve was an old hand at documentary-making, having made almost 50 docos with his wife Terri. The day he died, it was just a normal working day. Only it was nothing of the sort.

Out on Batt Reef, off Port Douglas, Irwin's 22-metre, double-deckered research boat, *Croc One*, was more than well-equipped to handle the day's work. Impressively custom-crafted (designed by Steve himself), it had two floating crocodile traps, an inflatable dinghy, two shark dive cages and two cranes for lifting heavy creatures from the water. And if that wasn't enough, there was also room for a helicopter.

The documentary they were making was ironically called *Ocean's Deadliest*, a 26-part series for US cable TV. But the weather wasn't on their side that day and poor conditions led to frustrating breaks in production. During one such break, Steve just couldn't help himself. Why sit around when he could get some action? So he thought he would put in some extra time and get some good footage for his daughter Bindi's up-coming TV show.

There were plenty of giant stingrays around that morning, some more than two metres across. Steve had his pick. He singled out a big black one known as a bull ray and got closer. The camera rolled. The water was shallow, only about 1.5 metres deep. Steve swam alongside the giant ray, with the cameraman in front, filming its mesmerising rhythm.

And then Steve swam over the top of it. With Steve on one side and the cameraman in front, the ray most likely felt under threat. It went into defensive mode. Suddenly it stopped, turned and made an upwards swipe with its barbed tail. Steve was right in its path. The jagged knife-like barbs ripped his chest open and speared him close to his heart. Steve frantically pulled at the barb as blood began to stain the water. The cameraman stopped filming.

The distress call went out at 11.21am. Within a couple of minutes, the film crew had hauled Steve back on to *Croc One*. And then began a futile attempt to revive him. His ribs were slashed and he had a gaping wound near his heart.

Emergency Management Queensland told the crew to meet a helicopter at Low Isles, about 30 minutes away. The boat got there at about 11.50am with crew giving him CPR all the way in a desperate attempt to save his life; the helicopter arrived soon after. Many snorkellers nearby were absorbed by the emergency but had no idea who was on board. Steve had no pulse. He was not breathing. The emergency doctor recognised almost instantly that there was nothing he could do. Steve Irwin was pronounced dead.

In the moments that followed, there was absolute silence. A marine biologist on board echoed the thoughts of so many when he said, 'These things don't happen, the guy's invincible, and there he is, we had lost him, he was gone.' (*The Courier Mail*, p. 1, 6 September 2006).

At first, it was not known whether Steve had died of a heart attack, blood loss, venom or a combination of all three. It was most likely not the poison that killed him, but the effect of the barb in his flesh. The barb would have punctured his heart or severed a major artery, resulting in fatal blood loss; an effect similar to that of a knife or spear plunging into the chest.

The news spreads

Within 30 minutes of the news appearing on *The Sydney Morning Herald's* website, smh.com.au, it was the day's most viewed story. The ABC news site crashed before returning with a home page solely devoted to the story everyone wanted to read. News of his death quickly topped Google News, which tracks 45,000 news sources. The BBC's live internet monitor had a 50 per cent increase in traffic and Steve Irwin-related searches filled the top three places on Technorati, which tracks 53 million blogs. Steve's death was the lead story on all the main US news websites.

Terri Irwin and the two children were having a hiking holiday in Cradle Mountain, Tasmania, when she heard the news. Just after 5pm that day, they boarded a private plane and headed back to Queensland.

Even before Steve Irwin's body was flown from Cairns back to the Sunshine Coast, the gates of his Australia Zoo were transformed into a huge shrine as well-wishers covered the ground with stuffed toys, drawings, candles and flowers. His funeral was telecast live in Australia and the US, and tributes took place against a giant backdrop of Steve's trademark grinning face. Even in death, Steve Irwin proved to be larger-than-life.

Did you know?

Jeff Zahmel was only 12 years old when he became the first official recorded stingray fatality in Australia. It was March 1988. Jeff was with his dad, his brother and two friends in a dinghy crossing Mourilyan Harbour at Innisfail in far north Queensland. A light wind was blowing. The boys moved around to distribute their weight evenly in the dinghy; Jeff moved to the centre. Out of the blue, a stingray leapt from the water, soaring over the dinghy. Three of them felt it brush across them and probably that contact put the stingray on alert. So its reflex action was to whip out its barb and pierce whatever came its way. Which just happened to be Jeff's chest.

Jeff stayed overnight in hospital as a precaution then got the all clear and went home. The only evidence of the bizarre happening was a small roundish mark on his left nipple. But six days later, he went for a walk with his dad along the beach at Tully. He came home as his mum was getting lunch. He sat down, said he just wanted an Easter egg and his brother yelled out, 'Mum, Jeff's gone funny' (*The Australian*, p. 1, 6 September 2006). It was as instant as that. Jeff Zahmel was dead.

2.
Beach

The beach is a strong part of the Australian identity but many overseas visitors are oblivious to its dangers. Drowning is the third biggest cause of death of international tourists in Australia after natural causes and car accidents; and sharks don't always attack a long way offshore. In this section, you'll find three shark attack stories all linked by a common theme: all three victims were swimming in the shallows. First up is a vicious attack on a young woman at North Stradbroke Island; then a boy attacked by a shark that would not let him go; and the poignant story of the young actress who became the last known shark attack victim in Sydney Harbour. Finishing the chapter is the cautionary tale of a recent arrival in Australia who drowned at Bondi Beach on his 42nd birthday. If only he had swum between the flags ...

SHARK

THE YOUNG WOMAN WHOSE ARMS WERE RIPPED OFF

Name:	**Sarah Whiley**
Age:	**21 years old**
Nationality:	**Australian**
Incident:	**Shark attack**
When:	**7 January 2006**
Where:	**North Stradbroke Island, Queensland**
Outcome:	**Fatal**

North Stradbroke Island is a popular spot for holiday-makers, with its deep blue freshwater lake, swamp wallabies, rare golden wallabies and a myriad of native flora including beautiful wild orchids. 30 kilometres SE of Brisbane, it's Queensland's most easterly island which means it's a place where northern and southern ocean currents meet. This, in turn, brings in a great variety of fish and where there are fish, there are sharks. The locals know it; and they've known it for a long time. But day trippers are often not so aware. Which is exactly the scenario with this tragic story.

Perfect conditions for sharks

The relentless whirr of the shark patrol helicopter is a reassuring sound up and down the Queensland coast on weekends and public holidays. From its base on the Gold Coast, the chopper does regular aerial patrols of popular beaches and islands as far north as the Sunshine Coast. It regularly sights sharks and gives warnings for beaches to be cleared. The search helicopter flew over North Stradbroke Island's Amity Beach regularly but not daily. It flew over on 6 January and 8 January, 2006.

But not on Saturday 7 January.

It was overcast on that particular Saturday afternoon. There'd been a big storm the night before and pelting rain had churned up the shallow waters and made them murky. There were a lot of bait fish in the water, like tuna. The dolphins swam amongst them, nudging them into shoals. Where little fish are, big fish will follow. And then you'll get sharks. On any day, if you head up to the headland at Point Lookout, the island's main beach, you'll see them.

There were bull sharks around that time of year. Bull sharks, or bull whalers as they're also known, have stocky bodies, rounded snouts and can weigh over 100 kilograms. They are thought to be particularly aggressive but that could be because they've had a lot to do with humans. Bull sharks feel at home in exactly the same watery environment that humans like: the warm shallows. They travel extremely fast; they have attacked people in water less than knee-deep and they have been known to eat dogs.

Amity Beach is not the island's safest beach. It has a short stretch of shallow water and then there's a sudden drop into Rainbow Channel, one of the deepest channels in Moreton Bay. It's the place where the ocean flows into the bay, the entry point for sharks looking for bait fish. The locals sometimes refer to it as 'Shark Alley'.

The row of drum lines at Rainbow Channel is intended to keep sharks away. Nets aren't much use because of the strong currents and the huge tidal variation. Cynics would say drum lines aren't much use either. Drum lines are a series of floats with an anchor attached. A cable runs between an anchor and a float and there are baited hooks strung along the cable. But bait attract small fish and small fish attract big fish and so it goes …

Oblivious to the danger

Late on that Saturday afternoon, a group of young people from a holidaying Brisbane church group decided to go for a swim. Among them was Sarah Whiley, who was 21 years old. She was a third-year occupational therapy student from McDowall, a northern suburb of Brisbane. The spot they chose was about 500 metres north of the swimming enclosure at Amity Point jetty. There were a lot of people on the beach that day. Late afternoon, overcast, warm current, run-off from rain. Lots of food about for sharks. Conditions like these made locals more than wary, so much so that they wouldn't even consider swimming at that particular spot. But visitors don't know this. All they see is an idyllic swimming spot, warm and inviting. When this fellowship group decided to go for a swim, they were putting themselves in grave danger without even realising it.

Sarah Whiley swam out of the shallows into the deeper water of Rainbow Channel where buoys mark the drum lines. It was 4.50pm. She turned and started swimming back to shore. She was in waist-deep water with a couple of friends about 20 metres from the shore when she was attacked.

The attack was sudden and vicious. In a matter of moments, the shark or sharks ripped off both her arms in a frenzied assault. She disappeared under the water. Five or six seconds later she resurfaced, gasping for breath and screaming, 'Shark!' At first, everyone thought she was joking. But then blood, too much blood, began clouding the water.

The friends who were only metres away swam frantically to her rescue. Two fishermen reacted quickly and calmly, dragging Sarah onto the beach, being tracked by the sharks as they did so. With a sudden aggressive attack it's hard to be sure how many sharks were involved. The brutality of the attack was just beginning to sink in: 'I went to grab her arm,' said one horrified eye witness, 'and her arm wasn't there ...'

After Sarah was pulled from the water, the immediate concern was her huge loss of blood. Beach towels were padded up against her in a frantic effort to try and stop the flow of blood. Emergency services were quick to respond. Sarah was carried up the slope to the ambulance in a stretcher. The ambulance sped to the oval next to the community centre where a helicopter arrived to take her to Princess Alexandra Hospital in Brisbane.

Her injuries were horrific: massive blood loss, loss of both arms and major injuries around the torso and legs. She died 90 minutes after arrival.

Locals agreed that given the weather and surf conditions that day, a shark attack was virtually inevitable.

Sometimes it's harder than you may think to establish exactly what kind of shark is involved in an attack. Or even how many sharks there were. Despite the number of witnesses, the attack on Sarah Whiley was so sudden that there was confusion about what kind of shark attacked her. Some locals believe it was a lone tiger shark. Others think that there were probably up to three bull sharks.

CSIRO scientists examined shark teeth fragments from the scene. There wasn't enough DNA to prove conclusively that it was a bull shark but bite patterns and teeth fragments indicated that it was the most likely candidate. The strong feeling was that more than one shark was involved, but there was no way of proving that conclusively.

Back in the water

One week later, swimmers were returning to the spot where Sarah Whiley was killed. Even though lifesavers strongly advised them to stay away, adults, toddlers and dogs were splashing in the water just metres from where the attack took place. A local teenage boy stood and looked at them, appalled: 'It's the stupidest thing I've ever seen,' he said, echoing the thoughts of many.

A poignant reminder of a life taken remains: scattered flowers, a letter from Sarah's friends and a silver crucifix attached to a tree washed up on the beach.

THE SHARK THAT WOULDN'T LET GO

Name:	**Raymond Short**
Age:	**13 years old**
Nationality:	**Australian**
Incident:	**Shark attack**
When:	**27 February 1966**
Where:	**Coledale, NSW**
Outcome:	**Non-fatal**

Sharks—like all other creatures—flourish in certain environmental conditions and have distinctive patterns of behaviour. What is so interesting about this shark attack is that the shark's behaviour didn't make any sense at all. It was swimming in shallows when it should have been in deep water; and even after it was dragged out of the water and carried up the beach, it refused to let go of the victim's leg. It simply didn't add up to normal shark behaviour. Lifesavers who heard the poor boy screaming, 'Get it off! Get it off!' thought he was just in shock—until one of them reached down under the water and felt a shark's snout still firmly clamped to the boy's leg.

A caravan park weekend

February 1966. Summer was nearly over but the days were still perfect for the beach. 13-year-old Raymond Short was having a weekend away with his mum and dad, George and Lesta. They had driven south from Hurstville, a southern Sydney suburb, and were staying in a caravan park at Coledale, about 60 kilometres south of Sydney. The family may well have expected to spend their weekend looking for shells, getting a bit sunburnt and playing some beach cricket. But they certainly wouldn't have expected their son's dramatic rescue story to be plastered all over the front page two days later with headlines like: 'Shark Savages Boy in Coledale Beach Drama', 'Men Carry Shark Victim to Beach', and 'Boy, 13, Held By His Legs'.

Sunday afternoon was warm and balmy. The coastal patrol plane flew over. No sign of sharks. A little after that, at 2pm, Raymond went in for a swim. He waded into the water in the patrolled area of the beach where there were about 60 other swimmers. The water was murky, just like the day before, and there was lots of seaweed in the water. But seaweed is a common sight up and down the coast and no one thought anything of it. Until Raymond screamed.

The boy must be panicking about being caught in some seaweed. That was the first reaction from most of the lifesavers on the beach that day. After all, he was only about 30 metres from the shore in waist-high water.

A patrol member who was in the water at the time, rescuing another swimmer, saw what appeared to be a clump of seaweed drifting towards Raymond, then heard the boy yell. Another lifesaver sitting on the edge of the water heard people yell, 'Shark!' and thought it was a joke. Even when he saw the boy bobbing up and down in the water, the lifesaver's first thought was that he must be caught in a rip.

So he jumped into the water and swam out to help; four other lifesavers plunged into the water too. Then one of them saw an ominous shadow in the clouded water: the outline of a shark. And the water around Raymond began to turn red. According to one unsubstantiated report, Raymond bit the shark on the nose and said it was like 'hard old salty canvas'. He could taste his own blood. A wave broke and washed the struggling pair closer to shore.

By the time the first lifesaver got to Raymond, there was no sign of the shark. He reassured him, 'You're all right now, son.' But the boy couldn't be comforted, crying, 'Please help me. It is still on my leg.' And he kept up his cry, 'It's still got me. Get him off!' Knowing how shock victims can behave, the lifesaver held him tight, lifted him up and did his best to reassure him again: 'You're all right, son. I've got you—the shark has gone away.'

But then he reached down under the water and, to his horror, felt something. The unmistakeable body of a shark … still clinging desperately to Raymond's right leg!

The determined shark

A nearby surfer offered his board as a stretcher and they made good, pulling him in to shore. Since the shark wouldn't release its grip, they figured they'd have to drag it in. So two of the rescuers grabbed the 2.5-metre shark by the tail and began to haul it towards the shore. One young lifesaver ran into the water and smashed the shark over the head with a surfboard. But to no avail. Raymond was helped onto the sand, while four lifesavers managed to lift the shark from the water and carry it up the beach. It must have been a sight to see that afternoon: a schoolboy and a shark carried in tandem onto the sand.

The enthusiastic lifesaver tried again, hitting the shark over the head with the surfboard. But the shark still refused to unclamp itself from Raymond's leg despite being punched, kicked and banged on the head! In desperation, one of the lifesavers ran home to fetch a rifle but it proved unnecessary. While he was gone, the others managed to prise open the shark's jaws. Finally, it loosened its grip on poor Raymond.

The boy was badly mauled. Surf club members applied tourniquets to both his legs and wrapped him in a blanket. They rushed him to nearby Coledale Hospital in the back of a station wagon where doctors were standing by. He was conscious all the way. Just after Raymond arrived, an ambulance arrived with blood serum and albumen to stem the effects of shock and loss of blood. Hospital staff got one of the lifesavers to speak to him, to reassure him that the shark which had attacked him was most definitely dead.

The ambulance took off again, this time to collect more blood from Wollongong and Bulli Hospitals. Raymond was badly injured. Both his legs were torn and his hands were badly lacerated from trying to fight off the shark. He had several blood transfusions and underwent a gruelling two-hour operation. When he left the operating theatre, he was still in a critical condition with doctors unable to say whether his leg would need to be amputated or not. Meanwhile, two of the lifesavers involved in the rescue became violently ill and were treated for delayed shock.

Happily, the next morning amputation was deemed not necessary.

It was touch-and-go but over the next couple of days, Raymond's condition improved.

What type of shark was it?

The shark that wouldn't let go became the subject of great interest in marine circles. Shark researchers were intrigued by its appearance and its unusual behaviour. Newspapers of the day declared it to be a blue-pointer. But on examination, it was found to be a 2.5-metre female white shark about five years old, weighing 136 kilograms. A female of this age would most usually be found in clear deep water, that is, water more than six metres deep. So what was it doing lurking in murky shallows?

Its appearance gave a fair share of clues. On its sides were deep gashes and vicious teeth marks, believed to be recent wounds from an attack by a larger species such as a tiger shark or bull shark. It also had shrivelled skin which indicated it was in an emaciated state. All in all, its lack of a good feed and its wounds made it a rather sorry specimen, quite possibly not physically strong enough to return to its natural environs.

So there were two possible reasons why it stubbornly wouldn't let go of Raymond's leg. One, it was in a such a state of starvation that its body was shutting down and the muscles of its jaw just couldn't function properly any more. Or, two, it was so desperate for food that nothing would induce it to give up its chance for a feed—not even being dragged up a beach and whacked on the head with a surfboard.

THE LAST SHARK ATTACK IN SYDNEY HARBOUR

Name:	**Marcia Hathaway**
Age:	**32 years old**
Nationality:	**Australian**
Incident:	**Shark attack**
When:	**28 January 1963**
Where:	**Middle Harbour, Sydney, NSW**
Outcome:	**Fatal**

'Shark kills actress in shallow cove: fight by fiancé,' screamed the headlines of *The Sydney Morning Herald* on 29 January 1963. 'Woman killed by shark' was the lead story for *The Daily Mirror* the same day with a gripping follow-up story on page two suggesting that the 'killer shark may attack again'.

The victim was a well-known Sydney actress. The attack was in surprisingly shallow water, just above knee-height. And it all happened in a charming little bay in Sydney Harbour, sending chills down the spines of locals and tourists alike. And yet, while the fear of shark attack is a primal response to a genuinely dangerous threat, the chance of being attacked in Sydney Harbour needs to be put in perspective. Marcia Hathaway was attacked by a shark more than forty years ago—and there has not been a shark fatality in the harbour since.

A jaunt on the harbour

It was a lazy Australia Day long weekend in 1963. Seven friends were out on a cabin cruiser, an 8.5-metre vessel named *Valeeta*. Among them was Marcia Hathaway, a 32-year-old Sydney actress, and her fiancé Frederick Knight, 38. The *Valeeta* was anchored about 20 metres off Sugarloaf Point in Middle Harbour. Four of the group went ashore, while the other three remained on board. Sandra Hayden and James Delmege went looking for oysters on the rocks, while Marcia and Frederick dived overboard and went for a swim in the shallows. They were splashing and frolicking six or seven metres from the shore when suddenly Marcia screamed.

Out on the rocks, James heard the scream, but thought nothing of it, presuming it was a playful squeal. Marcia herself didn't yet sense the great danger either, telling Frederick she thought she'd been stung by an octopus. Then a second piercing scream rang out. In an instant, James was sprinting to the water to help. The water was bloody and foamy. Marcia was thrashing and struggling. Frederick was kicking at a shark, trying to trying with his bare hands to get it to release its grip on Marcia's leg.

The shark had bitten Marcia below the calf. With its second lunge, it almost tore her leg from her upper thigh. 'It seemed like 10 minutes to me while we struggled,' Frederick later recounted, 'but it could only have been a couple of minutes. The water was stained with blood and I never thought I would get her away from it. I think at one stage I had my foot in its mouth. It felt soft and spongy.'

Frederick didn't get a close look at the shark. But he later remembered standing and straddling it with the shark's body touching both his legs. So it must have been a fair size. Frederick and James dragged Marcia up onto the sand. Frederick tried to reassure her, playing down the severity of her injuries. But he knew that she knew.

Meanwhile, the friends on the boat reacted quickly. They grabbed some sheets, jumped in the dinghy and rowed to shore. Using the sheets as tourniquets, they applied the makeshift bandages as best they could. Mobile phones hadn't been invented yet; they had to get to the nearest phone. There were houses backing onto the water about 700 metres away but they were not visible from the beach. So the group transferred Marcia into the dinghy, rowed back to the *Valeeta* and sailed around to Mowbray Point where there was a boatshed at the bottom of Edinburgh Road, Castlecrag. While Frederick dived overboard to ring for an ambulance, the others got Marcia to shore in the dinghy.

When the ambulance arrived minutes later, Marcia had lapsed into unconsciousness. Ambulance officers used oxygen to revive her and got her into the ambulance. The slippery surface conditions and the steep grade of the road combined to make the journey uphill impossible. Of all the things to happen, the ambulance's clutch burnt out. An old black and white photo shows a group of 20-30 people, including Frederick, desperately trying to push it up the hill.

A newspaper reporter at the scene radioed for a second ambulance but Marcia Hathaway died from shock and loss of blood just 20 minutes later. 'I have seen men die but I have never seen anyone so brave as Marcia,' Frederick Knight later said. 'When I asked her if it hurt much she said, "No, I am not in pain". I think the last words she said to me were, "Don't worry about me, dear. God will look after me."'

Afterwards, the owner of the Castlecrag boatshed said that a couple of dogs had been taken by sharks in the area the week before and that he had seen two large sharks in the bay earlier that morning. From teeth fragments found, the shark was identified as a medium-sized whaler. The public was warned to stay out of the water as it was possible the shark would strike again somewhere else in the harbour.

Frederick Knight never got to make his special announcement. Sadly, he had intended to announce their engagement formally on Marcia's birthday, 8 February, less than two weeks after her death.

Did you know?

Max Rowley, the well-known radio broadcaster, had the unenviable experience of discovering his friend Marcia had died while reading the news on air on 2CH. 'The first piece of newscast didn't give a name,' he said. 'Then I saw the second slip with the name Marcia Hathaway on it. I don't know how I managed to read it over the air.' Marcia was well-known from the long-running radio serial *Blue Hills*, and she had been working on a TV serial for children, *Smugglers Beware*, at the time of her death. A plaque inside St Stephen's church in Macquarie Street, Sydney, reads: '... in memory of Marcia N. Hathaway, actress and devout Christian, victim of shark attack in Middle Harbour 28/1/63.'

DROWNING

A BRIGHT FUTURE ENDS AT BONDI BEACH

Name:	**Yondon Dungu**
Age:	**42 years old**
Nationality:	**Mongolian**
Incident:	**Drowning**
When:	**20 January 2007**
Where:	**Bondi Beach, NSW**
Outcome:	**Fatal**

It's conceivable that the man you're about to read about didn't know the full story about Sydney beaches. After all, he was from Mongolia, a country devoid of coastline, sandwiched between the great sprawling nations of China and Russia. He'd left Mongolia to start a new life with his wife and three children and the future was looking good. He was set to start full-time study, get permanent residency and bring his children up in the Land of Opportunity. Everything was falling into place. Nine days after the family flew into Australia, it was his birthday. To celebrate, they took an afternoon trip to Bondi Beach for that quintessential summer experience. But in the blazing hot summer sun, his bright future became engulfed in darkness.

Wild weekend weather

The weekend of the 20 and 21 January 2007 was a scorcher. Sydney beaches were packed with day trippers; conditions were rougher than normal. At Coogee, three people were taken to hospital with neck and back injuries after being dumped in rough surf. At Little Bay near Malabar, a 33-year-old man drowned. At Bondi, a similar tragedy was about to unfold. But for the moment, the bright afternoon sun couldn't suppress a sense of optimism.

It was a stunning day, with a sparkling sea and seagulls squawking, a scene locals knew and loved. There were families there, toddlers in their sun-resistant lycra zip-up suits and caps, Bondi Icebergs stalwarts jogging along the shore, backpackers kicking back and bleached surfers who surfed every single day. But there was one family there to whom all these sights and sounds were new and exciting. This was only their second weekend in Australia and they'd come to Bondi Beach to celebrate their dad's 42nd birthday.

Yondon Dungu was a doctor who had first glimpsed what life in Australia could be like in 2000 when he came to Sydney to study for a Masters in Health Administration at the University of New South Wales. He loved what he saw: a bright future for the taking, broadened work opportunities and a good education for his three children. He was a gentle, loving man who took his role of breadwinner seriously. After the death of his eldest brother, he had become the head of the family and main provider for his nine younger siblings, a responsibility which he took in his stride.

When he completed his Masters and returned home to Ulan Bator in 2002, he set about making his dream reality. Four years later, he was accepted as a full-fee-paying student back at his old stamping ground, the University of NSW. He decided to retrain as an accountant with the aim of getting permanent residency and raising his family in Australia.

In early January 2007, the family arrived: Dungu, his wife Tseggy, sons Zorig and Batcha, aged 16 and 11, and daughter Soinbayer, aged 14. They had poured all their life savings into this major move, feeling positive that they were embarking on a bright new phase of their lives. They picked out a modest flat in Rosebery and the children were enrolled at Randwick Boys' and Randwick Girls' High Schools. It was a Sydney summer: full of sunshine and optimism.

Going for a swim

At about 5pm, Dungu went in for a dip at South Bondi about 100 metres from the Icebergs pool. Although air temperatures were high, the ocean was colder than average for the time of year. An hour went by. And then another half hour. By 6.45pm he still hadn't come out of the water and the family grew concerned, worried that he'd been in the surf too long. They went and found some lifesavers.

An immediate search failed to find any trace of him. Soon after came the unmistakable sounds of a sea rescue chopper doing a low aerial search. Everyone on the beach looked up; everyone knew they were looking for something. Or someone. And then a surfer out in front of the Icebergs Club suddenly signalled back to the squad on the beach. He had found what the helicopter had failed to locate: Yondon Dungu floating face down about two metres below the surface of the water.

The beach was cordoned off for more than half an hour while the painful and distressing rescue operation swung into action. Lifesavers hauled Dungu out of the surf, using a jet ski with a board on the back. They carried him up onto the sand where paramedics straight away commenced CPR. His distraught family were treated for shock while the gruesome scenario played out right in front of their eyes. A waiting ambulance sped him to St Vincent's Hospital, but Yondon Dungu was already dead.

The Bondi Beach lifesavers were shattered that day; they were used to saving lives, not lives being lost. Dungu's death deeply affected many and the local community rose up to give their support. The local council, police who'd been on the scene and a coalition of local licensed venues paid for Dungu's funeral. The University of NSW's School of Public Health, where Dungu had studied, set up a trust fund which raised tens of thousands of dollars for the family in the first week. Dungu's wife, Tseggy, expressed her gratitude for such generosity. But Dungu's children never did get to start at Randwick Boys' and Randwick Girls' High. The new furniture for their spartan flat was never delivered. Tseggy and the three children returned to Mongolia.

Did you know?

The day after Dungu drowned, two young women were left bereft in Sydney's southern suburbs. It was a red hot Sunday afternoon, the temperature reaching 41° C. At Sandringham Bay, two happily in love couples were having a picnic. The two young men, Ali Ibrahim, 20, and Samir Chakik, 25, were both recent arrivals in Australia. They were planning to marry two Sydney sisters later that year, 20-year-old Zeinab and 22-year-old Fatima Ibrahim.

At 3pm, the men headed off to a popular swimming spot near the wharf. They were not the strongest of swimmers and they wouldn't have realised that although the water is only shoulder-deep, it runs off into a deep channel with a strong current. Pretty quickly, Ali got into trouble and Samir jumped in to help. Other swimmers valiantly came to their aid, including one exhausted man who had only minutes before pulled his 13-year-old son and another woman to safety. In the 15 minutes it took for police and an ambulance to arrive, the men had disappeared. A massive search began; a rescue helicopter even dumped coloured dye in the water to gauge the pattern of ocean currents. It wasn't until early Tuesday morning that the first body was found, floating 200 metres offshore in Botany Bay. The second body was found the following day by a fisherman about 300m east of Bestic Street, Kyeemagh. The girls' father was faced with two unenviable tasks: consoling his bereft daughters and contacting the men's relatives in Lebanon. And the two sisters were left to identify their fiances' bodies.

3.
Seashore

Australian seashores have a wealth of riches: intricately patterned shells, sea green rock pools, hermit crabs and brittle stars. Cone shells may look exquisite but some are lethal to humans. Puffer fish contain a deadly toxin. And the blue-ringed octopus, a pretty little creature especially attractive to children, is capable of causing paralysis and death. In this section are three tragic stories all involving death by these seemingly innocuous sea creatures.

There's the story of a young army recruit who goes for a walk on the beach during his lunch break and 90 minutes later is dead; the tale of two young lovers who run away from home only to die horribly from puffer fish poisoning; and the story of a young man who unwittingly becomes the first cone shell fatality in Australia.

CONE SHELL

It's easy to think of shells as things rather than animals, and passive things at that. The cone shell is anything but. If you can imagine a snail with the ability to shoot out venomous darts just like a blowpipe, that's the kind of extraordinary creature the cone shell is. Its darts are hollow, barbed and very deceptive: they not only fire forward, but can whip around and shoot from any part of the shell. That is why cone shells should never be handled.

If the prey is particularly tricky to catch, the cone shell will pump extra venom into it through its dart until it finishes it off. Then it drags the victim back into its snout using the barbed dart like a harpoon. Most cone shells live on marine worms and molluscs but the larger shells can spear fish. These are the ones that are most dangerous to humans. Among these is the geographer's cone—*conus geographus*—a species that is quite rare. The geographer's cone has a macabre claim to fame: it is responsible for the one and only known fatality by a cone shell in Australian waters, way back in the 1930s.

THE MAN WHO SHOULDN'T HAVE PICKED UP A CONE SHELL

Name:	**Charles Garbutt, aka 'CHG'**
Age:	**29 years old**
Nationality:	**Australian**
Incident:	**Cone shell**
When:	**26 June 1935**
Where:	**Hayman Island, Queensland**
Outcome:	**Fatal**

The place is Hayman Island in the Whitsundays. The time is the mid 1930s. What should have been a glorious day out turned to tragedy because no-one at the time realised how deadly cone shells were. No-one sought medical help until it was too late. No-one was aware of how time was running out for a certain young man. This is the story of that man, out on a pleasure cruise for the day, who picked up a cone shell and five hours later was dead.

Tropical paradise

In these days of slick marketing, the Whitsundays are synonymous with all that is luxurious about tropical resort holidays. It's not just the rich and famous who get to go there; the islands are readily accessible to corporate clients, couples and families through a bewildering array of package deals and discount online air fares. But in the 1930s, the chance to go to the Whitsundays was a special event and a cruise to Hayman Island—the northern-most island, closest to the Great Barrier Reef—was a rare treat. That's what gives this particular story such poignancy.

A cruise set out on 27 June 1935 to spend the day sailing around the Whitsundays. On board was a young man who would long after be known only through medical reports as 'CHG'. World-wide to date there have been sixteen recorded deaths by cone shells. 'CHG' made medical history by becoming the one and only known victim in Australian waters.

His name was Charles Garbutt and he was 29 years old. He came from a well-known Townsville family and was a keen footballer in peak physical condition. Out for a day trip with family and friends, nothing could be more perfect. The tropical waters were crystal clear, the sandy shores of the isles they visited were dotted with an abundance of shells.

The cruiser was on its way back home when it made its last stop at Hayman Island. A group from the boat went out on the reef, collecting shells. Charles saw a most magnificent specimen: *conus geographus*, the geographer's cone.

Cone shells are highly prized by shell collectors; this particular species even more so because of its rarity. It can measure around 13 centimetres in length and weigh up to two kilograms, substantial dimensions for a shell. They are also much admired for their intricate patterning of browns, oranges and creams. Some look like snake skins, some look like old weathered maps. The trick is that they are often covered by an outer layer or epidermis which needs to be scraped off to reveal the full beauty of the shell. Charles followed his instincts. He picked up the cone shell, placed it in the palm of his hand and, with the other, began scraping off the outer layer with a small pocketknife to reveal the exquisite pattern beneath.

Almost immediately, Charles Garbutt noticed that his hand had begun to lose feeling. Numbness descended to the point where he couldn't feel his hand at all. But the strange thing was, it didn't hurt. Within ten minutes, Charles' lips felt stiff and he complained of a burning sensation around his mouth. But still, he was feeling no pain. After 20 minutes, the next terrible symptom took effect. His vision started to get blurry. Half an hour after the sting, he found he could no longer walk. His legs were paralysed. Half an hour later, Charles Garbutt lapsed into unconsciousness.

No-one was alarmed

These days, the scenario would be very different. Long before he was unconscious, someone would have whipped out their mobile phone and dialled 000 for medical help. Emergency first aid would have commenced, a doctor would have arrived and an airlift to hospital would have given him valuable time in his fight for life. But no doctor was called. The strange thing was that no-one was especially alarmed. Even though Charles was unconscious, he continued to breathe normally and everyone thought he'd pull through. The ship's captain later explained that his companions said he had recovered from similar 'turns' twice before. They didn't realise that this 'turn' was different.

By the time the cruiser reached Cannon Valley, it was dark and Charles' condition was growing worse by the minute. He was now in a deep coma. A doctor was called and Charles was transferred to an ambulance which sped to hospital. It was 6pm. By now, almost five hours had passed since he had held the beautiful cone shell in his hand. His pulse became weak and rapid, his breathing became laboured. Tragically, he died just as the ambulance reached the hospital.

For all the wrong reasons, Charles became a cause célèbre. His case made the illustrious pages of *The Medical Journal of Australia*: 'The victim was prior to the injury in perfect physical condition and in training for football.' (4 April 1936). The official finding was heart failure due to toxaemia. And the only visible trace of the exquisite but deadly cone shell was a tiny puncture mark on the palm of his hand.

Did you know?

Bruce East from Exmouth in Western Australia knows what it's like to be stung by a cone shell. But fortunately for him, he lived to tell the tale. In February 1988 he was diving with his wife Aileen in Light House Bay, off North West Cape in Western Australia. He found two specimens of *conus geographus* and hung them on his diving belt in a mesh bag. Cone shell darts can penetrate fabric so a mesh bag wasn't much protection. Bruce was stung but didn't know it—not until an hour later when the first effects took hold.

First came weakness and disorientation; then his breathing became erratic. 'My eyes felt like leaden balls. My legs felt like I had run a marathon,' he later recalled (*The Age* 25 July 2005). He managed to struggle ashore and Aileen drove him to hospital quick smart. Luckily for Bruce, his wetsuit was a true lifesaver. The fabric hadn't stopped the sting reaching his skin but it had stopped it penetrating too deeply. The worst was over within five hours, but for days after Bruce still had difficulty sleeping and concentrating.

PUFFER FISH

'Poisonous' and 'venomous' are used interchangeably but, strictly speaking, an animal is venomous if its bite does you serious damage and poisonous if eating it kills you. Puffer fish are poisonous. Their toxin is impressive: more toxic than cyanide and one tenth of a gram is all it takes to kill a human being. Since the first puffer fish death in Australia was recorded in the *Sydney Gazette* of 1821, more than 15 people have died from the effects of its poison, a poison which has been identified as tetrodotoxin, or TTX for short.

Its modus operandi is gruesome: it works by slowing down all normal bodily sensations and movement. Muscles, heartbeat, vision, ability to speak—all shut down and death eventually comes from asphyxiation. The worst part is that the victim remains fully conscious and lucid throughout but is physically unable to communicate. Current medical thinking is to just keep respiratory and circulatory systems functioning until the effects of the poison wear off; to date there is no known antidote to TTX.

THE TWO YOUNG LOVERS AND THE SPOTTY FISH

Name:	**Phillip John Cartledge**
Age:	**23 years old**
Nationality:	**Australian**
Incident:	**Puffer fish**
When:	**29 August 1965**
Where:	**Eden, NSW**
Outcome:	**Fatal**

Name:	**Jocelyn Jean Jones**
Age:	**19 years old**
Nationality:	**Australian**
Incident:	**Puffer fish**
When:	**29 August 1965**
Where:	**Eden, NSW**
Outcome:	**Fatal**

This is the story of the irrepressible optimism of youth, of a young couple who ran away together to find happiness: camping under the stars, swimming in crystal clear waters and living on bounty from the sea. But they were inexperienced in the ways of the world and instead of simple pleasures the pair found suffering and death. They didn't realise that fishing is harder than it looks, or that the spotty fish they caught were no good for eating, and in fact were highly poisonous. They had run out of money and were desperate for food. They cooked the fish over a fire and ate them. And the rest is history …

The idealism of youth

Phillip Cartledge grew up in Tasmania, the oldest of three boys. He joined the Army when he was seventeen and served for six years, including a two-year stint in Malaya. After leaving the Army, he took up a job as a psychiatric nurse at Lachlan Park Hospital (later the Royal Derwent Hospital) in New Norfolk, Tasmania. And then he met Jocelyn Jones and fell in love.

They were young, idealistic and inseparable. They had no plans; they just wanted to be together, to travel and be free. So they ran away. They took off in their old model Holden, caught a boat to the mainland and escaped. Police would later find that they arrived in Melbourne on the Princess of Tasmania on 21 August 1965.

It was a big adventure for the pair but a great surprise to their friends and families who were unaware of the couple's plans to elope. Jocelyn lived with her grandmother, who didn't know anything of their plans. Phillip's mum and dad didn't know whether they were on holiday or whether they intended to return to Tasmania or not. All they got was a letter from Phillip asking for money to be sent to the post office at Bairnsdale, Victoria. Phillip's dad sent the money but it was never collected. A bad omen.

It seems that the two decided to drive up the New South Wales coast and start a carefree life together, living day-to-day, swimming in the sea and catching fish. But by the time they got to Eden, on the NSW south coast, their dream life was not so dreamy. Their money had run out and they took to camping in their car overnight. They had nothing to eat and their petrol tank was running on empty. It was only a little over a week since they had left their homes, but already they were in desperate straits.

On 29 August 1965, Phillip and Jocelyn left their car and walked along a bush track for more than three kilometres to get to the beach. They caught some fish and ate them then began walking back to the car. But Jocelyn became sick, too sick to keep going. So Phillip left her and kept heading down the road on foot to get help.

A slow kind of numbness

On the way, Phillip started feeling ill himself, a slow kind of numbness. He met a timber worker who stopped a passing car and asked the driver to get medical help. Reportedly, Phillip muttered, 'My wife is back there and needs help.' (*The Sun*, p. 23, 31 August 1965). The men dashed back along the track and found Jocelyn lying there, passed out. The driver then rushed Phillip to the nearest doctor, Maurice Waters in Eden, who later reported, 'Cartledge staggered out of the car … he was partly paralysed and told me he had been eating spotted fish he had caught near a beach four and a half miles north of Eden …' (*The Mercury*, p. 1, 31 August 1965).

Gasping for breath, Phillip managed to describe the fish: small, about 15-20 centimetres long with tough skin and spots on their back. But he didn't make it into the surgery. A few minutes later, he collapsed and died in the doctor's arms on the front lawn.

The man who had brought Phillip into town told the doctor about Jocelyn Jones. So Dr Waters jumped into his car and went searching. He found Jocelyn, lying dead on the bush track. Beside her was a rucksack containing fishing lines, hooks, a small frying pan and some cooking utensils with fat on them. Their old model Holden with Tasmanian number plates was about 800 metres away. Inside was a small tin of sugar, another frying pan and four shillings: all they had left in the world.

The cooking utensils were sent to Sydney for analysis. Autopsies revealed that the two young lovers died from puffer fish poisoning. And Jocelyn's family were left with her last words so bright and optimistic: 'Dear Mum and Family, Phillip and I are going to get married. Please don't worry, everything will be all right ...' (*The Sun*, p. 23, 31 August 1965).

Did you know ...?

Death from puffer fish has also happened in more recent times. In May 2007, the ship's doctor on a Chinese iron ore carrier, *Tian Yang Hai*, died a horrible death from eating puffer fish. The ship *was anchored* off Dampier, Western Australia. The doctor caught a puffer fish and kindly shared it with another crew member. They both began to feel ill, starting off with an uncomfortable numbness of the tongue and lips which rapidly turned to dizziness. The crew member made himself vomit to get rid of the toxin. The doctor couldn't and found himself in the throes of paralysis in the middle of the night, unable to move his arms or legs. He called for help.

While waiting for Australian Search and Rescue, a third member of the crew began mouth-to-mouth on the doctor, only to become ill himself with numbness of the lips and tongue. By the time help arrived, the doctor had stopped breathing. He was taken to Karratha Hospital but died there the following morning. The crew member who had selflessly performed CPR on the dying doctor was also taken to hospital. Happily, he recovered.

BLUE-RINGED OCTOPUS

The blue-ringed octopus is a seemingly innocuous little creature, hardly what you'd call a giant of the sea. The two species that occur in Australian waters range from about 12-20 centimetres from top to toe, that is, from the top of their head to the end of their tentacles.

When sitting on a rock minding its own business, the octopus is a dull brownish colour with streaks of pale blue. But when it senses danger, the dull colours darken and the pale blue turns an amazing iridescent blue—hence the name. The blue-ringed octopus is extremely venomous. It has a tiny parrot-like beak and when it bites it injects toxins in its saliva. It has a paralysing effect on its victims through the deadly component tetrodotoxin (TTX), a similar modus operandi to the puffer fish. The Aborigines knew the blue-ringed octopus was dangerous. But Europeans weren't really aware of it until the mid-twentieth century; 1954 in fact.

THE SOLDIER, THE SAILOR AND THE OCTOPUS

Name:	**Kirke Dyson-Holland, aka 'Dutchy'**
Age:	**21 years old**
Nationality:	**Australian**
Incident:	**Blue-ringed octopus**
When:	**21 September 1954**
Where:	**Darwin, Northern Territory**
Outcome:	**Fatal**

Name:	**James Albert Ward**
Age:	**23 years old**
Nationality:	**Australian**
Incident:	**Blue-ringed octopus**
When:	**23 June 1967**
Where:	**Camp Cove, Sydney Harbour, NSW**
Outcome:	**Fatal**

'Navy man dies after octopus bite' read the front page of the *Northern Territory Times* on 21 September 1954. 'Octopus kills aoldier' cried *The Sydney Morning Herald*'s front page 13 years later on 23 June 1967. The headlines tell it like it is. This is an account of the only two recorded fatalities of blue-ringed octopus in Australian waters so far. The first fatality was in tropical Darwin; the second in downtown Sydney in a harbourside haunt that is nowadays better known as a nudist beach. Sadly, both deaths were of young men who didn't do anything particularly reckless; they simply let the octopus come into contact with their skin, not realising its capabilities. Strangely, both were military men: a young sailor and a young army recruit inducted only the day before his death.

The off-duty sailor

The story begins in Darwin in the mid 1950s. Able Seaman Kirke Dyson-Holland—known to his mates as Dutchy—was 21 years old. He left his hometown of Yuroke in Victoria and was posted to Darwin on HMAS *Melville*. There he joined the Arafura Skindivers' Club. One day when he was off-duty, he decided to go spearfishing with a friend, Frederick John Baylis. They chose a spot off East Point, where Darwin's War Museum now stands.

They were heading back to shore when Frederick Baylis noticed a blue-ringed octopus about 20 centimetres long swimming around in ankle-deep water. Both men had handled them before and thought they were harmless. Kirke said that it would make good fishing bait. So Frederick picked it up—he recounted later that it was red and green—and let it crawl over his arms, shoulders and chest. And this way, they waded back to shore.

On the shore, Frederick saw some coral he was interested in, so he asked his mate to mind the octopus for him while he had a look. Kirke was loaded up with fishing gear, so Frederick tossed the octopus onto his shoulder. It crawled over him, just like it had done on Frederick's back. 'I was walking behind Dutchy,' Frederick recounted, 'when I saw the octopus stop still for a few seconds on his back, high up and close to the spine. Then it dropped off.' (*Northern Territory News*, p. 1, 21 September 1954).

Frederick picked up the octopus again and tossed it back into the water. Shortly afterwards, Kirke told him that his mouth was dry and that he was finding it difficult to breathe, but neither of them was particularly concerned. Kirke did not realise he had been bitten, which is common as the bite is painless. This also makes it frightening because it means a bite can go unnoticed until it's too late. Soon, the full effects of the tetrodotoxin kicked in. Kirke felt nauseous, vomited and began staggering around the beach. He collapsed, which was when his friend noticed the trickle of blood from the tiny puncture on his back.

Frederick carried him across the beach; others ran to his aid and helped get Kirke back into the car. They sped off to Darwin Hospital. The trip was just over five kilometres but on the way Kirke stopped breathing and his skin turned blue. At the hospital he was given oxygen and put in an iron lung. Many resuscitation attempts were made but failed. Two hours after the bite, Kirke Dyson-Holland was dead. And the post-mortem could find not a trace of a bite mark on his skin.

Later, Frederick Baylis caught an octopus that he thought was the same species that had killed his friend. It was wrongly identified as *octopus rugosa*, a common kind of octopus known for having a bite like a bee sting. In 1964, the case was re-examined and the venomous octopus was found to be *hapalochlaena lunulata*, the northern species of the blue-ringed octopus.

One lunchbreak ...

The second recorded death from a blue-ringed octopus in Australia was of another young military man, this time a soldier. Private James Ward was with two other army recruits exploring rock pools at Camp Cove, near the Naval Base at Watsons Bay in Sydney Harbour on 23 June 1967. He was at Watsons Bay for his induction into the Army and went exploring during his lunchbreak with two fellow recruits, Stephen Arthurson and Michael Novak, both 18.

They found an octopus in a rock pool and poked at it with a stick to see whether it was dead or alive. It was alive. They decided to take it back to the barracks to show their mates, so James placed it on his arm. But on the way back, he started feeling strange. He found to his horror that he couldn't get it off. He tried to vomit, but he couldn't, such was the creeping paralysis of muscles that had already begun.

His two mates tried to help him towards the Army Medical Centre, but he could only stagger about 10 metres. A sergeant told them to get James onto a bed in the barracks while he rang for transport to the Centre, which arrived within minutes. One of his friends finally yanked the octopus off and threw it away. But James was unable to swallow and was having great difficulty breathing. His breathing failed, he lost consciousness and five Army doctors commenced resuscitation during the wait for the ambulance.

Resuscitation attempts continued on the way to hospital in the police-escorted ambulance and again at Prince Henry Hospital at Little Bay, but to no avail. Forty-five minutes after admission and only ninety minutes after picking up the octopus, James Ward was dead. And as in the previous story, there was no trace of a laceration on his skin. Following his death, the Commonwealth Serum Laboratories examined the southern species of the blue-ringed octopus—*hapalochlaena maculosa*—which is slightly smaller than the northern species. Its venom proved to be just as deadly.

Tragically, James Ward had been inducted into the Army only the day before: a raw recruit to the end.

4.
Suburbia

S nakes, spiders and creepy crawlies are a big part of the Australian psyche; everyone's heard about the red-back on the toilet seat. The surprising thing is that tourist fatalities from snakes and spiders are exceptionally rare; it's nearly always the locals who get bitten and it's nearly always in deepest, darkest suburbia. These stories are about two men—one bitten by a death adder, one by a funnel-web spider—whose lives suddenly spiral into major medical emergencies.

SNAKE

ustralia is the only country in the world where there are more venomous than non-venomous snakes. But it's important to put this in perspective. Out of about 140 species of land snakes and 32 species of sea snakes, roughly 100 of these are venomous. But of these, only 12 are really likely to cause human fatalities. These include the eastern brown, a notably aggressive snake; the western brown; the mulga or king brown snake and the death adder. Even Australia's very own inland taipan, considered the world's most toxic snake in terms of the potency of its venom, has never actually killed anyone because it lives in such remote regions. Every year there are about 32,000 reported snake bites in Australia but only one or two fatalities.

BITTEN FIVE TIMES BY A DEATH ADDER

Name:	**Bruce Campton**
Age:	**51 years old**
Nationality:	**Australian**
Incident:	**Death Adder**
When:	**12 October 2006**
Where:	**Wisemans Ferry, NSW**
Outcome:	**Non-fatal**

Death adders don't fit the stereotypical image of a snake, if there is such a thing. They don't slither and hiss, they stay put and strike. They're not long and sleek. Quite the opposite. With their triangular-shaped head and squat body they look comical rather than efficient, but efficient they are. They're perfectly designed for attacking unsuspecting prey with a lightning-quick strike, using their prettily coloured tail as bait.

Most snakes slither around actively searching for food and just as rapidly slither away when a human approaches, but not the death adder. It remains in one spot, burying itself in sand if possible, waiting for prey to come: a habit which makes them particularly dangerous to unsuspecting humans. Since most snake stories happen to locals, here's one to warm the heart. This is the story of a man having a weekend away with his brother-in-law. He sees an unspecified creature in semi-darkness, mistakes it for a harmless blue-tongue lizard, gets bitten, goes into cardiac arrest and spends eight days in hospital. And after all that, he comes out smiling.

The man who loved blue tongues

Bruce Campton had a soft spot for reptiles, especially blue-tongue lizards. He had a bit of a reputation for rescuing poor defenceless creatures in all kinds of sticky situations. Like the time he stopped the car and dashed across a couple of lanes of traffic to rescue a bearded dragon that happened to be sitting pretty in the middle of a highway.

So when Bruce went off to have a break with his brother-in-law Colin, they picked a nice bushy spot: Del Rio water ski resort, a caravan park at Wisemans Ferry about 60 kilometres NW of Sydney. It was sure to have some interesting wildlife, poker machines and beer on tap as well. On that particular Thursday night, he'd had a good run at the pokies and pocketed $40. The two men were heading back to their cabin, ready for a barbecue, when Bruce saw a feral cat swiping and hissing at something on the pathway. He took it to be a poor old blue-tongue and ran to its rescue.

In the semi-darkness, all Bruce could make out was something short and stumpy. He picked it up and felt two sharp pin pricks on his hand; the ungrateful creature had bitten him! He managed to scoop it up and get it away from the cat, but the nasty thing bit him again and wouldn't let go. Bruce carried the tenacious little creature back to his caravan, prised it off his hand and dropped it into an empty beer carton for safe-keeping. That's when warning bells rang, at least for Colin, who diplomatically said, 'Campo, that doesn't look like a lizard. It's got no legs.' (*The Daily Telegraph*, p. 9, 4 November 2006)

It's not a blue-tongue, Bruce

Bruce reached down into the carton and felt along the body. He confirmed that indeed it had no legs, but not before it had bitten him yet again. At this point, Colin decided that it must be a snake and took off to fetch the bloke next door. Quick smart, the neighbouring holidaymaker burst in, took one look and let out a horrified cry: 'It's a bloody death adder!' (ibid).

Now, at this point, most people would be breaking out in a cold sweat, reaching for their pulse or running round the room screaming. Not Bruce. He just shrugged, commented that he didn't think death adders were found so far south, and asked for a smoke and a beer.

But seconds later, as he tried to twist the top off his stubbie, all he felt was a pins and needles sensation in his hands and feet. The bloke from next door must have sensed something was wrong. He grabbed Bruce's beer, just as the chair he was sitting on tipped over and Bruce fell backwards onto the floor with a crash. His head was spinning, he was sweating and struggling. Next thing, he couldn't move and someone was shining a torch into his eyes.

Bruce slipped in and out of consciousness. His head and hands were showing disturbing signs of swelling. His system was shutting down. He remembers the weird sensation of hearing people talking about him without knowing that he could hear them. He remembers tubes being shoved down his throat. He remembers hearing the paramedics cry, 'He's arrested!' and he remembers thinking, 'No, I haven't!' In his venom-induced haze, strange thoughts floated around his head: What if they think I'm dead? Will they bury me alive? Will I have to scratch myself out of my coffin? (*That's Life*, p.12, pacificmagazines.com.au).

The residents of the caravan park called an ambulance and the Careflight rescue helicopter. Bruce did, in fact, have a heart attack but was revived by ambulance officers before the helicopter arrived. The Careflight team took half an hour to stabilise him before air-lifting him to Westmead Hospital in critical condition. Meanwhile, quick-thinking bystanders had killed the snake and put it in a plastic bag so it could be identified by hospital staff. And, yes, it was a deadly death adder. In the Emergency

Department, Bruce was injected with massive doses of antivenom. He vaguely recalls medical staff arguing about whether to give him a fifth dose or not, just to be on the safe side.

Happy ending

Happily, Bruce lived to tell the tale. He was transferred to Intensive Care and left hospital more than a week later, pumped to the eyeballs full of antivenom. So much so, that the doctors warned him not to get bitten again; his body just couldn't take another dose for at least ten years.

Did you know?

For some strange reason, a lot of snake stories come out of Melbourne. You would think that living in this fair southern city would keep you out of harm's way. But in 2003, an elderly woman died after being bitten by a tiger snake while pruning the ivy in her garden in Kew, an inner city suburb. Two years later, a cyclist fell off his bike near the Yarra River in North Melbourne and landed on top of a very angry brown snake or tiger snake, the shocked man wasn't sure which. Naturally, the snake gave him a good bite, but his friends had the presence of mind to wrap his arm in an inner tube, cutting off the spread of venom through his circulatory system and saving his life.

Melbourne even has 'Snakebusters', a team ready to respond to snake sightings throughout the city. They have removed snakes from Fitzroy, St Kilda and Yarraville; one of their more interesting jobs was the removal of a literature-loving tiger snake from a bookshop in the Melbourne CBD.

SPIDER

Australia is home to two deadly arachnids: the red-back and the Sydney funnel-web. The red-back—*latrodectus hasselti*—is found Australia-wide, has body the size of a pea and has a distinctive red spot on its back. It's active in warm weather and loves dark, dry places like letter boxes and garden sheds. Its method of attack is to bite and run, leaving the victim with a venom that attacks the nervous system. By contrast, the Sydney funnel-web—*atrax robustus*—has a fast-acting venom. They are big, black and hairy and, because their fangs can only strike downwards, rear up on their back legs to make the hit. They live in the coastal Sydney region with Australia's highest population, and are found under rocks, inside a gumboot, up a shirt sleeve or under a pillow.

Funnel-webs and red-backs have been responsible for about 15 recorded deaths each, although the actual number is probably higher. The discovery of antivenom has made an incredible difference to the rate of spider bite fatalities in the country. Since red-back antivenom was introduced in 1956, there has only been one fatality. Since funnel-web antivenom was first used in 1981, no-one has died of a funnel-web bite, but the fear lives on.

THE MAN WHO DIDN'T DIE FROM A FUNNEL-WEB BITE

Name:	**Gordon Wheatley**
Age:	**49 years old**
Nationality:	**Australian**
Incident:	**Funnel-web spider**
When:	**31 January 1981**
Where:	**Sydney, NSW**
Outcome:	**Non-fatal**

This is the story of a man who should have died from a funnel-web bite, but didn't. He was the first person in the world to receive the antidote to the Sydney funnel-web, an experiment that thankfully worked. Although clearly not planning to be bitten, his timing was impeccable. Just six months before, Dr Struan Sutherland—who had been working on an antidote for 14 long years—finally showed that his antivenom reversed the effects of funnel-web poisoning in monkeys, the only other mammal known to be affected by the venom.

Three months before Gordon Wheatley was bitten, Dr Sutherland's ground-breaking results were published in the *The Medical Journal of Australia*. Fifty days before Gordon was bitten, the first experimental batch of antivenom was flown to Sydney because, after all, that's where the most lethal funnel-webs live. And just thirty days before he was bitten, the very first batch of antivenom was approved for manufacture. It's no exaggeration to say that without that antivenom, Gordon Wheatley would very likely have experienced agonising muscle spasms, slipped into a coma and died.

Suburbia

11pm in the leafy northern Sydney suburb of Cheltenham. Gordon Wheatley had just completed one of those mundane household chores—changing the light globe in the dining room. He was wearing socks but even so, as he stepped down from the stool, he felt a sharp prick on the sole of his foot, something like a drawing pin. As he shook his foot, he saw a spider scuttling away under a chair. He felt pain shoot up his leg and he knew enough to realise he'd been bitten by a funnelweb.

Luckily, his neighbour happened to be a doctor who knew what to do. He bound the foot with a pressure bandage—a treatment which was ahead of its time—and bundled him into the car. Gordon's son leapt into the driver's seat and the last thing Gordon remembers of the drive is his neighbour telling his son to 'go like hell!' (*The Sydney Morning Herald*, p. 3, 1 April 2006).

Gordon's son took the doctor's advice. They were at Ryde Hospital in 15 minutes but, in that short time, Gordon was already sweating profusely and getting palpitations. He was conscious. His pulse was up to 100 beats a minute and the muscles in his arms were starting to spasm. It was not a pretty sight: he was starting to turn blue and his whole body was jerking, tossing from side to side. He was put on an intravenous drip but he was thrashing around so much that he pulled it out. He couldn't keep his oxygen mask on either. His mouth had a tingling sensation, he was still dripping sweat and his skin was covered in goose bumps.

Hospital staff prepared for the worst. They knew what funnel-webs do. They knew the gruesome scenario and it went something like this: terrible muscle spasms making the skin go up and down in undulations like a woman's belly at the start of labour; goose bumps and profuse sweating. Gordon Wheatley had already shown these symptoms. But there was more to come. Next would come uncontrollable weeping and excessive salivating until watery white fluid was expelled from the lungs in a gross cascade of vomit. His blood pressure would plummet and there would be nothing anyone could do. He would drown in his own fluids.

Shortly after midnight, Gordon was sedated and rushed to another nearby hospital, Royal North Shore. His pulse was racing at 155 beats per minute, his pupils were dilated and not responding to light.

Medical staff knew but Gordon's wife, Gwen, wasn't really aware of how critical the situation was. As soon as she got to the hospital, the staff bombarded her with question after question. All she wanted to know was why she couldn't see her husband.

The human guinea pig

Dr Fisher was on duty that night. He explained that there was a new treatment—an antivenom—developed by Dr Struan Sutherland who had spent 14 years working on it. But they needed Gwen's permission to administer it because they had no guarantee of the side effects. In fact, the antivenom had never been used before on a human. Gwen asked the doctor what he would do if he was in her shoes —he would try it, he said. So she gave her permission. Her husband was injected with antivenom. Gordon Wheatley became a human guinea pig.

One dose. Nothing. A second dose. A third. No change. It was 1.30am. The situation was critical. Dr Fisher rang Dr Sutherland in Melbourne, lashing out in desperation: 'I've given him three ampoules of antivenom,' he said. 'It hasn't killed him, but hasn't done any bloody good either!' (*The Australian*, p. 15, 23 November 1998)

Dr Sutherland replied calmly that the best thing was to give him another dose because nobody really knew how much was needed. Dr Fisher went back to work and half an hour later was back on the phone. This time there was unmistakable relief in his voice: 'Struan, you've just ruined a beautiful syndrome!' (ibid).

Within an hour, there was an amazing turnaround. The symptoms were reversed and, by morning, Gordon Wheatley was no longer on the critical list. After another overnight stay, he was able to go home. For the next three weeks, he suffered weakness and heavy sweating but otherwise made a full recovery.

Twenty years later, Gordon Wheatley rang Dr Struan Sutherland and said, 'Hello, it's Gordon Wheatley.' Without missing a beat, the irrepressible Dr Sutherland replied, 'Well how the bloody hell *are* you?' (*The Sydney Morning Herald*, p. 3, 1 April 2006).

Since 1981, more than 100 people have been given antivenom and no-one has died from a funnel-web bite, which should make Sydneysiders and visitors sleep a little easier in their beds.

Did you know?

Sadly, the last Australian to die from a Sydney funnel-web was a two-and-a-half year old boy named James Cully. It happened in January 1980, a year before Gordon Wheatley's miraculous recovery. The family was on holiday at Wamberal on the NSW Central Coast and were getting ready for a walk along the beach one morning. John Cully, James' dad, grabbed the children's tracksuits which were lying on the laundry floor. As he put James' tracksuit top on, James pulled his arm away and said, 'needle'. John thought that he must have felt a splinter. He didn't know it, but a funnel-web spider was hiding in the right sleeve of the jacket.

Five minutes later on the way to the beach, John Cully felt a spider on him. It had a big black body and short legs. He brushed it off, thinking it must have fallen from a tree. But about 15 minutes later as they returned to the house, James began vomiting violently and losing consciousness.

John Cully put two and two together and raced James to Gosford Hospital. He was immediately put on a respirator; and later transferred to Intensive Care at Royal Alexandra Hospital for Children in Sydney. He died three days later from lung and kidney failure. In *The Daily Telegraph* of 7 January 1980, the sad headline read, 'Funnel-web bite fatal for James'. And underneath was a story which ran, 'After 20 years of research, scientists have still not found an antivenene for a funnel-web bite ...' All that was about to change.

5.
Bush

The Australian bush is a mass of contradictions; it's inspiring, monotonous, evocative and frightening; full of fragrant eucalypts, jewelled spider webs and confronting wildlife. Here you will read some disturbing accounts of the dingos that are increasingly becoming a menace to tourists—especially young children—on Fraser Island. There's the story of a high-flying executive lost on an island for ten long days; a hapless tour guide's attempt to get his group out of Knox Gorge before nightfall in the remote Karijini National Park; and the freakish tale of a Queensland sugar cane worker who is stalked and attacked by that most extraordinary of birds, the cassowary. But first, the story of a British tourist who vanishes without a trace on Fraser Island until another British tourist chances upon his skull two years later.

CAUSE OF DEATH UNKNOWN

THE MYSTERY OF DAVID JOHN EASON

Name:	**David Eason**
Age:	**46 years old**
Nationality:	**British**
Incident:	**Cause of death unknown**
When:	**Missing 28 March 2001; found 14 April 2003**
Where:	**Fraser Island, Queensland**
Outcome:	**Fatal**

A British tourist named David Eason disappeared on Fraser Island in 2001 and was never seen again. Until—by sheer coincidence—another British tourist came across his skull in 2003. This extraordinary discovery came after two years of fruitless searching during which Eason's family didn't let up in their criticism of the investigation. How could a man simply vanish? Why did the police give up so soon?

At the same time, Queensland's tourism industry had another horror case to deal with: a nine-year-old boy mauled to death by a dingo on Fraser Island (See 'The Dingos That Attack Children', this chapter). Naturally, the media took this up with great gusto which led to an unhealthy amount of speculation about whether David Eason had met a similar fate. In the end, the police investigation got a big rap over the knuckles from the State Coroner who found there had been some serious errors of judgement made. Indeed, from beginning to end, this whole story is marked by speculation, dissatisfaction and false theories that lead to nowhere but a gruesome end.

Holiday in Oz

Fraser Island, on the southern tip of the Great Barrier Reef, is the largest sand island in the world. It's famous for its white beaches and amazing array of coloured sands. There are over 100 freshwater lakes dotted across the island as well as rainforests and heathlands. It's also famous, or infamous, for its dingos. The dingos on Fraser Island have the purest gene pool of all the dingos in Australia. On top of all this, its natural wonders have given it World Heritage status which means it's a popular tourist haunt for Australians as well as overseas tourists.

In 2001, a British tourist named David Eason was staying at the Kondari Resort in Hervey Bay, 300 kilometres NE of Brisbane. The 46-year-old lived in Battersea, Greater London, and was Creative Director and part-owner of a company in Buckinghamshire that specialised in campaigns for the pharmaceutical industry. David had a girlfriend, Jo, was well-off, creative, loved swimming and sailing.

He was in Australia for a four-week holiday. He visited friends in Melbourne, travelled north to Sydney and then joined a 14-day tour heading up the coast to Queensland. The plan was to go to Cairns and enjoy some snorkelling on the Great Barrier Reef. On their way north, they stopped off at Fraser Island for the day.

28 March. The group caught a boat across Hervey Bay to Fraser Island to spend the day exploring the sand dunes and beaches in a four-wheel drive. At 1pm, they stopped on the eastern side of the island at a surfing beach at One Tree Rocks, about six kilometres north of Eurong Resort. Five of the party decided to take a look at the beach. They arranged to meet back at the car park near Lake Wabby at 3pm. From there, they would head back to Kingfisher Bay Resort on the other side of the island. Four of them set off along the 1.5 kilometre walking track to the meeting point. David Eason stayed behind to have a cigarette and told them he'd have a half-hour sunbake and then get going.

By 3pm, David Eason hadn't arrived at the meeting point. The group waited an extra hour for him to show. He never arrived and he never returned to his room at the Kondari Resort. He had vanished.

Missing

The tour company notified police and park rangers just after 6pm. A small ground search was conducted immediately and the next morning aerial sweeps failed to find any trace of him.

Police were puzzled by the disappearance. Words like 'bizarre' and 'baffling' were thrown around. The problem was that it seemed utterly implausible that someone could get lost on Fraser Island. Every day, tourists criss-crossed the island on well-worn walking tracks from beach to car park and back again. And so, early in the investigation, police looked to other, more complex, scenarios to try and explain his disappearance. The horrible irony is that if they had simply assumed he was injured and needed help, he may have been found alive.

In his hotel room, David Eason's passport and personal belongings lay untouched. However, letters were found revealing that he was not entirely happy with the tour or the weather, and he had a cold coming on. So one of the first scenarios the police looked into was that he had left the island. The tour leader said that David was a solitary man looking for time out and a change of direction in his life, but fellow tourists painted a different picture. They said he'd given no indication of wanting to leave and that he seemed to be looking forward to the next phase of the tour: snorkelling on the Great Barrier Reef. His neighbour back home in Battersea said there was no reason why he would disappear.

Three days after he was reported missing, David's sister, Janice Eames, flew in from the UK. She didn't like the sound of the police line of enquiry at all. She had last heard from her brother when he rang from Melbourne, telling her he was happy and enjoying his holiday. If he had wanted to disappear why join an organised tour? To her, his disappearance was totally out of character.

Another possible scenario was that David had drowned. The beach he had stopped at was treacherous with signs warning about undertows and sharks. But the weather wasn't great that day and the sea was rough. It was unlikely he'd choose to swim in those conditions and, besides, there would have been some trace of him left on the sand: his backpack, his sandals, the dark green singlet he was wearing. Foul play was another theory which became more plausible as time went on. Had he been robbed and murdered as he walked through the bush? Had he been struck by one of the four-wheel drives that roar up and down the beach, in a hit and run? Was he buried somewhere in the sand? All these theories were raised with varying degrees of conviction.

A helicopter using infra-red heat-seeking equipment searched the area but found nothing. The search was called off after a week with grave fears held for his safety. Posters of David Eason were put up on Fraser Island ferries and tourist spots over the Easter weekend, hoping that someone might come forward with information. The only useful lead they got was of a possible sighting of a man fitting his description on Thursday 19 or Friday 20 April, but this was a dead end.

On 30 April, nine-year-old Clinton Gage was mauled to death by a dingo on the island. This only fuelled speculation and gave international media a gory new angle to the story. A US-based film crew flew to Queensland to examine the Eason case as part of a series called *Hunter and Hunted*. The resultant episode, 'Death Down Under', asked the question: was missing English tourist David Eason the first fatality in the turf war between humans and dingos on Fraser Island? As it happens, he wasn't, but the idea added spice to a stalled search.

Back in the UK, David's family went to the media in frustration over what they felt was a lack of focus in the search. *The Guardian* and *The Evening Standard* ran reports on the disappearance. The family also appealed to the British government, claiming that Queensland police wouldn't act unless ordered to do so by a higher authority. The British Foreign Office, consular staff in Brisbane and London, Interpol and UK police were all contacted.

The family wants answers

4 May. David's brother Peter and his brother-in-law Michael Eames arrived in Brisbane, wanting answers. They were briefed by two Queensland police

officers and two British consular officials. At this stage, they were prepared to accept that David may not have survived, but they were determined to find out what had happened to him. Like Janice Eames, they argued that the initial search had been called off too early. Suppose that David had broken his leg? It was estimated that someone could survive under such circumstances for up to five days. Why, then, had the search been abandoned so soon? Both men went to Fraser Island and retraced David's last steps. They came up with nothing.

An SES training exercise was scheduled on Fraser Island for the weekend the two men arrived. Following pressure from Peter Eason and Janice and Michael Eames, this was turned into a major search involving 120 SES personnel who did an intensive scour of two square kilometres around Lake Wabby.

But again the search found nothing. The mystery remained. How could a man vanish on an island? Why could police find no trace of him? Police and Eason's family felt that he was still on the island somewhere. But where?

14 April 2003. Arwen Heaton, a fellow English tourist, set out on the same walking track that David Eason had intended to walk, from the beach to the car park. She had a map with her which showed a walking track starting at the northern tip of Lake Wabby. She walked along the eastern side of the lake, looking for it.

She saw a track heading into the bush and followed it for several metres, but it didn't lead anywhere. So she retraced her steps. It was then, as she backtracked, that she saw a skull. It was at the bottom of a steep slope, near the base of a tree. Scattered within a six metre radius of the skull were many items: sandals, a swimming costume, shorts, a watch and a camera.

Dental records confirmed that the skull was that of David Eason.

Coronial inquiry

The Coronial Inquiry concluded that if he had followed the directions to the car park given to him by his tour guide he would indeed have ended up in the spot where his remains were found. It was likely that he had fallen down the steep slope after taking a wrong turn, since many things that he had been carrying were found scattered down the slope: pieces of a broken CD, a CD case, some tobacco and sunglasses. His skeletal remains showed signs of being gnawed after death, probably by dingos. But because of the time that had elapsed between his disappearance and the discovery of his remains, cause of death would remain unknown.

The Coroner's report raised significant failings in the search, echoing the criticisms of David's family who had flown back to Australia to hear the findings. The State Coroner Michael Barnes said while there was no suggestion that authorities had acted wilfully or recklessly with regard to David Eason's safety, there had been 'some serious errors of judgement'. A senior police officer didn't begin an intensive ground search until four days after David went missing. Trained search dogs were not used. The quality of interviews with the touring group and the delay in attaining them was inadequate.

And, finally, it was found that in the initial investigation police had only really considered four scenarios: murder, absconding, drowning and suicide. The Eason family's barrister made the point that evidence indicated that at no time did investigators think something had happened to David Eason on the track. Chillingly, the real possibility that he had become lost and injured had itself become lost.

DINGO

The dingo is Australia's largest carnivorous mammal and is found in every state except Tasmania. It is thought to be related to Asian and Middle Eastern wolves and, as a consequence, its scientific name has recently changed from *canis familiaris* (domestic dog) to *canis lupus dingo* (wolf). Dingos are scavengers by nature. They eat kangaroos and wallabies, with rabbits, rats, possums and marsupial mice sometimes thrown into the mix.

THE DINGOS THAT ATTACK CHILDREN

Name:	**Kasey Rowles**
Age:	**14 months old**
Nationality:	**Australian**
Incident:	**Dingo**
When:	**4 April 1998**
Where:	**Fraser Island, Queensland**
Outcome:	**Non-fatal**

Name:	**Jennifer Glandberger**
Age:	**2 years old**
Nationality:	**Norwegian**
Incident:	**Dingo**
When:	**4 April 1998**
Where:	**Fraser Island, Queensland**
Outcome:	**Non-fatal**

Name:	**Clinton Gage**
Age:	**9 years old**
Nationality:	**Australian**
Incident:	**Dingo**
When:	**30 April 1998**
Where:	**Fraser Island, Queensland**
Outcome:	**Fatal**

Name:	**Scarlett Corke**
Age:	**14 weeks old**
Nationality:	**Australian/English**
Incident:	**Dingo**
When:	**10 November 2004**
Where:	**Fraser Island, Queensland**
Outcome:	**Non-fatal**

Fraser Island is home to roughly 100-200 dingos and they are the purest strain of dingo in the country. The unique nature of this World Heritage-listed island means that interaction between people and dingos is different to anywhere else in Australia. Over the years, interaction has been possible, even encouraged, as tourists feed, photograph and even 'play' with dingos. Subsequently, dingos have lost their fear of people. Stories pour in about dingos stalking, biting or attacking tourists and every time an incident happens, the dingo is identified, tracked down and killed. And the debate is raised: why should we cull dingos? After all, they are in their native environment.

In this section, you can read four unsettling incidents involving children and dingos on Fraser Island. It's a chilling combination but the reality is that dingos go for the physically small and the vulnerable. There is the fatal attack of a nine-year-old boy in 2001; and the story of a dingo that pads into the hotel room of two little girls three years later. But first, the separate but coincidental tale of two little girls, camping at different locations on the island, both bitten by dingos on the same evening.

Dinnertime

Evening falls on Fraser Island. It's dinnertime for the humans, and for the dingos if they're lucky. Wherever there's campers, there's food, and the dingos have learned to hang around. Maybe someone will feed them, even though it's illegal and worth an on-the-spot $225 fine. If not, they'll grab what they can get: steaks, sausages, even a good lick at the congealed fat on the barbecue grills after everyone has gone to bed. Over time, the dingos have been building up their repertoire of what you might call 'challenging behaviours'; knocking over Eskies, tearing down tents and nipping at tourists' legs. It's not surprising that year by year dingos get more and more used to tourists, silently observing, becoming familiar with the places they go and how they get there. And the dingos become bolder.

In early April 1998, the Rowles family from Grafton set out for Fraser Island for a camping holiday with some friends. They'd been there before with their two boys. This time they were back with a new addition to the family: Kasey, their 14-month-old baby girl. They arrived early Saturday evening and were struck straight away by how many dingos were hanging around; definitely more than last time they were there. First things first, they picked a site for the tents and started unloading the car. While Alan Rowles got out the gear, his wife Sharyn spread out the picnic blanket. Kasey toddled happily round the tents. Soon the sausages were sizzling on the portable barbie and Kasey was sitting pretty on the picnic blanket.

At about 7.30pm the adults sat down to eat. Alan's friend Scott shooed a dingo away. It seemed unimportant, part of camping life on Fraser Island. But it was a warning. A minute later, Kasey screamed, not her normal scream, something much worse. Sharyn shrieked. Just two metres away stood a dingo, perilously close to their young daughter.

It all happened so quickly. An eerie crunching sound echoed through the night: the sound of the dingo sinking its teeth into Kasey's shoulder. Kasey began to wail. The dingo shook her like a stuffed toy and began to drag her across the sand towards the darkness. Sharyn ran at the dingo in full fight mode. It dropped its bundle and fled into the bushes.

Sharyn was bordering on hysteria from the shock. She grabbed Kasey, cradling her in her arms, in frantic relief. She carried her to where there was more light. In the light, she could see the dingo's legacy: scratches, bruising and a bleeding lip. The worst thing was the teeth marks, a nasty bite on her shoulder that had broken the skin. Sharyn clung to her little girl and burst into tears. Kasey was alive; all she would need is a tetanus shot.

On the other side of the island

That same night, a similar scenario was taking place on the other side of the island. Elisabeth and Patrick Glandberger from Norway were camping with their three children and some friends at Lake McKenzie. They were setting up their tent and one of their friends was about to take the children on a walk to collect some firewood.

Suddenly the eldest boy yelled 'dingo!'. Jennifer, the youngest, was only two and scared of dogs. She saw the dingo, turned and started to run, the worst possible response in the situation. The dingo sprang to the chase, caught her and knocked the screaming child to the ground. It gave her a nasty bite on the back of her leg before it was chased away. Another potentially fatal situation was averted; another terrified little girl needed a tetanus shot; another series of debates would rage about dingo culling on Fraser Island.

A draft strategy about dingo management on Fraser Island was released in May 1999 for public comment but after sifting through 35 submissions and numerous consultations with community groups, the final version only got to the Queensland Environment Minister in April 2001. By then it was too late. The worst had happened.

Stalked

April 2001, three years since Kasey Rowles was attacked near the barbecue. The Gage family from Brisbane was on a four-day holiday, camping at Waddy Point at the same camping ground chosen by the Rowles. It was Monday 8.50am. Nine-year-old Clinton and a friend wanted to go and explore the sand dunes nearby. They set off along the well-worn track that ran about 150 metres from the campsite, a track familiar to tens of thousands of holidaymakers.

The boys soon realised that they had company; they were being stalked by some dingos. Two dingos in particular took an interest in them, a female and a juvenile male. The boys remained calm and acted like there was nothing wrong, but the dingos were not going anywhere. They stuck close to the boys, silently watching.

It was unnerving. The two boys began to feel afraid. They made a run for it. But in their panic, they ran towards the sand dunes, not towards the safety of the camping ground. Clinton only got about 15 metres when he tripped and fell over. That was all the dingos needed. They pounced in a swift and vicious attack. Clinton's friend ran for his life, doubling back to the camp site to get help.

Clinton's dad, Ross, and younger brother Dylan, aged 7, rushed to the scene. They found Clinton lying mauled on the track, his major arteries severed. Instinctively, Ross wanted to shield his youngest son from the horror. He sent Dylan away, back to the campsite and, in disbelief, turned back to gaze at Clinton. But there was no time for grief. Suddenly Dylan screamed as a dingo leapt on him, toppled him over and went in for the attack. Ross kicked the animal away and comforted his bleeding son. Taking him in his arms, he carried him to where Clinton lay. But more horror awaited. In the few moments Ross had his back turned, the other dingo had sneaked back and now stood there mauling the boy's body. Ross picked up his dead son and trudged back to the campsite, carrying his two sons over his shoulders. Behind him, the most fearless of the two dingos padded along silently.

Stealth and silence

A British couple had a taste of how stealthy dingos are three years later. Belinda and David Corke were on holidays at Kingfisher Bay resort on Fraser Island with their five-year-old daughter Georgia and 14-week-old baby Scarlett.

Just before breakfast, the two girls were in their bedroom, when suddenly Georgia screamed. At first Belinda thought she was mucking around, but then David distinctly heard her shout, 'dingo, dingo!' They raced to the girls' room, expecting to see a dingo outside, perhaps on the balcony. But the dingo was in the bedroom.

Silently and swiftly, it had come in through the open doors on the balcony and pushed open the door to the girls' bedroom. It was standing less than a metre away from the sleeping baby. Little Georgia had placed herself between the baby and the dingo, the defiant act of a very brave big sister.

When Belinda came into the room, the dingo didn't move. It just looked at her. She shooed it away but it stood its ground. Only after David made a hullabaloo by stomping his feet and clapping his hands, did it turn and slowly pad away. Needless to say, the Rowles were shaken up that morning. They believe the dingo would have gone for their baby if not for the boldness of five-year-old Georgia. And the last word goes to Belinda, who was quoted as saying, 'I must admit the first thing I thought of was Azaria Chamberlain.'

LOST

THE HIGH-FLYING EXECUTIVE
LOST FOR TEN DAYS

Name:	**Ricardo Sirutis**
Age:	**48 years old**
Nationality:	**Colombian-born Brazilian resident**
Incident:	**Missing for 10 days**
When:	**Reported missing 9 May 2005; found 17 May 2005**
Where:	**Moreton Island, Queensland**
Outcome:	**Non-fatal**

This is the story of a high-flying business executive who does something that high-flyers don't usually do. He gets hopelessly lost on a sub-tropical island. As a result, a massive rescue operation springs into action: 500 SES volunteers, 77 army personnel, police, motorbikes, quad-bikes, four-wheel drives and helicopters are all out looking for Ricardo Sirutis. Finally, after ten long frustrating days, he is found semi-delirious, unable to move, but overjoyed to have someone to talk to. While recovering in hospital, he is able to tell his brother and the media the whole fascinating story: how he got lost, what he did and what it was like. His humour and fighting spirit is what makes this such an absorbing story of survival.

Day-tripper

A 90-minute catamaran trip from Brisbane will take you to Moreton Island, the second-largest sand island in the world after Fraser Island. The island boasts three small townships, five camping grounds and one resort as well as Mount Tempest, the highest stable sand dune in the world. More than 95 per cent of Moreton Island is National Park consisting of freshwater lakes, heathlands, wetlands and forests of scribbly gum and pink bloodwood. And there is 'The Desert', an enormous sand blow of 42 hectares of dazzling white sand. This is where our story takes us.

On the morning of Sunday 8 May 2005, staff at Legends Resort, Surfers Paradise, noted a South American guest browsing over brochures in the lobby before settling on a day-trip to Moreton Island. He checked in his suitcase and said he would return that same evening—only he wouldn't be returning for quite some time.

At about 1.20pm that day, a family from the Gold Coast was scurrying back to their hotel room on Moreton Island. There was a storm brewing. They said 'g'day' to a man heading in the opposite direction. The man they had seen was due to catch the 4pm water taxi from Tangalooma back to the mainland. He didn't show. And soon that Gold Coast family realised that they were perhaps the last people to have seen the man alive.

Ricardo Sirutis was due on the Gold Coast for a conference at the Sheraton Mirage Resort on The Spit on Monday 9 May. But on the Monday morning, the first day of the conference, he didn't turn up. Colleagues knew he was reliable. They contacted police.

Ricardo was no ordinary day-tripper. He was the Head of Consumer Division in South America for the pharmaceutical company, Pfizer. The conference he was scheduled to attend was a three-day meeting of Pfizer executives. He was also a keen bushwalker who often went exploring while travelling. This time, though, despite his experience, he was missing. A search commenced on Tuesday 10 May, with a search command set up at the Tangalooma Wild Dolphin Resort on Moreton Island. About 20 resort staff, 20 State Emergency Service (SES) volunteers, three police and four helicopters focussed on The Desert, two kilometres south of Tangalooma where he was last sighted.

After three wet and chilly nights, fears were growing for his safety. The rain was not helping him or the searchers. By this time, about 50 police and SES volunteers had joined the search. A couple of days later, Ricardo's brother, Stany Sirutis, flew in from Vancouver. The 54-year-old described his brother as fun-loving, cool-headed and physically fit with a strong survival instinct. Given such a wrap-up, it's not surprising

Stany was totally convinced that Ricardo was still alive, which was a great morale-booster for the search teams. Search numbers were ramped up considerably. As well as police, there were now about 100 SES personnel, paramedics, motorbikes, quad-bikes, four-wheel drives, rescue boats and helicopters involved.

All scenarios considered

Saturday dawned. And with it came clearer weather. The searchers were systematically covering The Desert, resorting to crawling on hands and knees, such was the terrain. The assumption was that Ricardo Sirutis had fallen and injured himself somewhere. But every other possibility, no matter how way out, was also considered. Had he been bitten by a snake? Taken by a shark? Drowned? There was mention of wild boars …

Other scenarios included the possibility that he had left the island or even faked his disappearance, although this was considered unlikely. Ferry passenger lists were followed up. Police investigated his background, building a character profile to try and make sense of his last known movements. He was single and cashed up with no known partner or dependants.

Monday 16 May. One week since Ricardo Sirutis was reported missing and still no sign of him. His brother vowed to stay on the island until he was found.

The next day, nearly 80 soldiers from Brisbane joined more than 500 SES personnel and police officers; this was a search on a truly unprecedented scale. The decision to search a new area—south of the original search site—was a good one. That afternoon at about 2.35pm, SES volunteers heard someone crying out. They yelled out several times until again they heard someone yell back. It sounded for all the world like, 'Hello, how are you?'

Ricardo Sirutis was sitting on top of a ridge, a mere three kilometres from where he'd last been seen. Shoeless, sunburnt and thirsty, he was unable to move. He was semi-delirious and so happy to see them he asked 23-year-old SES volunteer Katie Avery to marry him! It was important to keep his delirium at bay so they joked with him, asking if he'd like a beer. 'I'd love a beer,' he replied, 'we should go over to Brazil to have beer!' (*The Courier-Mail*, p. 1, 19 May 2005).

Ricardo was winched to safety and taken to Royal Brisbane Hospital by helicopter. He had lost 12 kilograms, his limbs were swollen and it was a miracle that he was still conscious. He probably wouldn't have survived another 24 hours given his low body temperature. But he did survive. Five days without water and ten days without food.

The two brothers were overjoyed to be reunited and Ricardo's rate of recovery was amazing. The next day when his colleagues came to visit him in hospital, he cracked them up by quipping, 'What are you guys doing for lunch?' (*The Courier-Mail* p. 6, 20 May 2005).

What happened

A couple of days later, Ricardo had recovered enough to tell his story. Ironically, his first choice for a day-trip had been Fraser Island, but it was booked out. So he went to Moreton Island after reading up about The Desert, the idea of which he found fascinating. Once there, however, the sheer scale of The Desert disoriented him. On that first Sunday, he tried to cross the sand and climb a dune on the other side. But he never made it. When darkness fell, he saw lights and a road that seemed close but were deceptively far away. He would see a light at the top of a dune and walk towards it, only to find nothing. He kept climbing up dunes, trying to use the beach as a reference point, but when he climbed down, he'd lose his bearings. In his semi-delirious state, he only remembered walking; he had no recollection of stopping or resting.

Ricardo believed the only thing that kept him alive was a big storm on Day Five that gave him the chance to gulp fresh rainwater spilling down from the leaves of a large eucalyptus tree. The leaves reminded him of his childhood home; there had been a small eucalyptus behind his house in Columbia. He tried to eat some but no matter how hungry he was, he just couldn't stand the taste. Apart from taste-testing the leaves, he ate nothing at all. He also remembers seeing a helicopter fly over and shouting and waving. But they didn't see him. And the spontaneous marriage proposal to the SES volunteer when he was rescued? Pure joy at being found. 'And the lady also was very nice,' he added, a joker to the end (*The Sunday Mail*, p. 2, 22 May 2005).

Since his ordeal, Ricardo Sirutis has looked at life differently and reaffirmed the value of his family and friends. He's kept in touch with his rescuers via email, telling them he'd love to come back to Moreton Island only this time with a GPS and Katie Avery as his guide! He believes few countries would have devoted so many resources to save one person. And he is probably right. The intensity of the search may well have been a reaction to criticism of the search for British tourist David Eason who went missing on neighbouring Fraser Island in 2001, and whose remains weren't found until 2003 (See 'The Mystery of David John Eason', this chapter).

And, finally, as an appreciative gesture, Ricardo's company Pfizer donated $50,000 to Queensland's Emergency Services. After all, a search operation costs about $4000 an hour.

THE TOUR OF KNOX GORGE

Name:	**Florian Bayard**
Age:	**29 years old**
Nationality:	**Swiss**
Name:	**Jill Cowie**
Age:	**23 years old**
Nationality:	**Australian**
Name:	**8 unnamed Japanese tourists**
When:	**Lost 12 June 2005; rescued 13 June 2005**
Where:	**Karijini National Park, Western Australia**
Outcome:	**Non-fatal**

This is the story of the fate of ten tourists, not one. There's the tour guide, a whining Swiss tourist who grows increasingly peeved as the drama unfolds, an Australian woman who fears she is going to die and eight young Japanese women.

Remoteness personified

Karijini National Park, North Pilbara. If you want remoteness, you've got it. It's Sunday night 12 June and the car park at Weano Gorge would normally be deserted. But a tour bus stands there. It has been parked there for much of the day. Four members of a tour group are waiting on the bus, getting anxious. Ten others from their group are supposed to have returned from their trip to Knox Gorge, but there is no sign of them. As darkness descends, the car park transforms into a makeshift command post. Police, ambulance officers, a park ranger and State Emergency Service (SES) workers from the closest towns of Tom Price and Newman have all converged to take part in a massive search operation. How can ten people and an experienced tour guide just vanish?

On Sunday morning, the tour group set off on an expedition to Knox Gorge. John and his son Dave were running the tour. The group was made up of mostly young Japanese women as well as a Japanese man, a

German woman, a Swiss man and an Australian woman.

They had wetsuits for swimming but even so the waterhole was unusually cold. From the bottom of the gorge, the quickest way out was to climb. There were metal rungs set into the sheer cliff face of the gorge for that purpose and there were also two rope ladders. The group successfully climbed the first of the rope ladders. Then they were offered the chance to make a daring plunge into the pool 14 metres below. There weren't many daredevils or adrenalin junkies among them; only three of them took up the offer. So John took off with the small group to enjoy leaping into the waterhole. Soon, one of them returned with bad news. The Japanese man had knocked himself unconscious doing a belly flop.

It was about 1pm when Dave made an emergency call for help. John decided the best thing would be for the group to continue their ascent and climb the second ladder. Florian, the Swiss man, looked up at the sheer cliff face and the second ladder. One of the rungs was broken. He had a bad feeling about the whole thing and didn't think that anyone would make it. He was almost right: only four of the group managed to clamber up.

The four that clambered up helped carry the 34-year-old Japanese man out of the gorge with Dave. So now the group was split in two: four who'd got out; the other ten who were left behind. It seems that those remaining were not having the greatest of bush experiences. They were still in their wetsuits, they had no shoes. All in all, they were cold, tired and hungry.

Stuck between two rope ladders is not quite the same as stuck between a rock and a hard place but the similarities were there. The group took a break and snacked on some apples and biscuits. Then John changed tack. He gave up trying to get them to go up; he decided to go back down. And so, somewhat unwillingly, they began their descent back down the first of the rope ladders.

The emergency crew arrived, ready to perform a difficult cliff rescue. They'd responded as quickly as they could. It's just that the Pilbara is a big place and they were based at Tom Price, two hours away by road.

Somewhere along the line, Dave was supposed to have cancelled the emergency crew, because by this time, the injured man and his helpers were well and truly out of the gorge.

The Japanese man had managed to climb back up to the top of the gorge with help from the other four tourists, despite suffering neck, head and chest injuries. He was taken to Tom Price Hospital by ambulance while others of the emergency team attempted to rendezvous with the remaining tour group. But there was no sign of them. And out there, satellite phones don't work too well.

Meanwhile, instead of keeping the group where they'd been left and waiting for help, John decided to try and walk out of the gorge. He walked, swam and waded the increasingly disgruntled group for almost four kilometres but it wasn't easy. Especially since four of them couldn't really swim, at least not more than 20 metres at a time. Our Swiss anti-hero Florian swallowed a lot of water along the way and started to feel sick.

At 5pm, the light started to fail. John tried to hurry them along, telling them they could still get out before dark. But the reality was hopeless. They were shivering in their wetsuits, their feet freezing cold. And you can't climb up a cliff face when your hands won't stop shaking. With the fading light, John decided it was too dangerous to proceed.

The search is on

Back up at the top, the tourists who'd got out safely from the gorge were waiting at the bus, wondering what was going on. They told emergency personnel that the rest of the group would be following them out, but clearly this wasn't the case. It's a good thing Dave's emergency call wasn't cancelled because police were already at the scene. When night fell and there was a 'no-show' by the rest of the group, the search was on.

Police had concerns because the group was unprepared for an overnight stay. They only had light clothes and wetsuits, no food or camping equipment. They would most likely be wet with no chance to dry off and the temperature was likely to drop down to four or five degrees Celsius during the night. Hypothermia was a real possibility.

It was not a group of happy campers who found themselves stranded for the night in a cold, dark gorge. They removed their wetsuits and put on their summer clothing. They found a big rock and tried to find somewhere comfortable to sleep on the ledge. They took it in turns to move around and huddle together to keep warm and at least retain some body heat. Florian had problems of his own; he was violently ill six times throughout the night. He was not impressed by this wilderness adventure-gone-wrong and would later describe it as one of the worst nights he'd ever spent.

Police called off the search at 8pm and resumed at 6am the next day with 25 police, SES volunteers and rangers.

The plan was to start at Joffre Gorge, the entrance to the gorge system, and work their way in from there. There were crew stationed at all the entrances to the gorge to cover all bases. It was rugged terrain so they figured the group would have stayed put overnight. Rescuers were hopeful they'd be found soon and, if not, they planned to start a helicopter search later in the day.

7am. The disenchanted group of ten was up and about. No injuries, just a strong desire to get out. They struggled into their wetsuits again to continue on their way. Did they know an emergency search was on? It seems unlikely because, as Florian later explained, if he had known there was a rescue team there the previous afternoon, he wouldn't have set off on a futile four kilometre walk/swim. He was not happy to continue walking; he was vomiting and experiencing double vision. Fortunately, his nightmare would soon be over.

About three hours later, the emergency crew found an encouraging sign: footprints. And then, just before 11am, there was a visual sighting of the group. The emergency crew was heartened to see them all walking. That meant no major injuries and no major logistical-nightmare-rescue-scenarios.

The long-suffering group was wading across a small pool when they heard shouting from above. It was the rescue team, asking if anyone was hurt and confirming that two of their men were coming up from behind. Florian's relief turned to deep annoyance when John insisted they keep going, forever onward, as if he didn't want them to be rescued at all.

Out of the gorge

They emerged from Joffre Gorge, cold, hungry and dishevelled. Mark McGowan, the Western Australia Tourism Minister, was there to witness their safe return and he commented, 'These people were physically exhausted—one of them told me she thought she was going to die during the night. It was so cold there this morning that it felt like you were standing in a snowstorm, and we had layers of clothes and were not in the gorge.' (*The Advertiser*, p. 9, 14 June 2005).

The ten tourists were given thermal blankets and taken by bus to Tom Price Hospital about two hours drive away. Their only injuries were mild exposure and sunburn. During his stay in hospital, Florian wrote a six-page diary about his experience and it wasn't a positive one. He maintained that John kept going when the rescue team made contact, as if he didn't want them to be rescued, a view backed up Port Hedland speech therapist Jill Cowie who said, 'I just feel that he wanted to get us out himself. He cared more about his own reputation than us and our safety.' (*The Australian*, p. 3, 15 June 2005).

The tour guide blamed officials for overreacting to the situation. He denied that he wanted to avoid the rescuers because he didn't have proper safety equipment for climbing the gorge. He insisted that it was better to keep walking than sit around getting colder. And he argued that the group was never in danger. But Jill (and assuredly Florian too) begged to differ, 'I thought we were going to die …' she said (*The Australian*, p. 1, 14 June 2005).

A state-wide review was conducted into safety standards for adventure tourism in Western Australia.

Did you know?

The tour group rescue was the third time in two weeks that police, park rangers and SES volunteers had been called out to search for lost people in Karijini. And there have been a string of other incidents too. One month before the Knox Gorge debacle, a 22-year-old German tourist fell from Hancock Gorge climbing down a ladder. She lay injured for almost 12 hours as emergency crews tried to reach her. Fortunately for her, she sustained only a broken wrist and a sore back. In April 2004, 36-year-old SES worker James Regan from Newman WA was swept away and drowned in a flash flood while rescuing a British tourist and an Irish tourist who had fallen from a cliff at Dales Gorge. He was the first SES officer to die in the 40 years of Western Australian SES operations. Two weeks after that, Dales Gorge was the scene of yet another tragedy when a 25-year-old man walking with fifteen others fell to his death.

CASSOWARY

Cassowaries are distinctively beautiful creatures. They have glossy cascades of dark feathers, rich blue markings on their necks and a bony cap on their heads called a 'casque', designed for forcing their way through dense forest. They are physically imposing birds with females growing up to two metres in height and weighing over 80 kilograms. They're an endangered species, with only an estimated 1200 left in three main populations in northern Queensland: two up in Cape York and the third stretching from Cooktown down to just north of Townsville.

The fascinating thing about these giant flightless birds is that they are capable of extreme violence. At first, if they feel uneasy, they'll make a low rumbling noise. Next, they'll express intimidation by a sharp hiss and irritation by noisy stomping. If cornered they will attack, leaping into the air with strange kick-boxing moves, running headlong at their victim and slashing viciously with the 12 centimetre tapering razor claws on their inner toes. This may in turn lead to massive bleeding, damage to vital organs and, in rare cases, death.

THE CASSOWARY VS THE SUGAR MILL WORKER

Name:	**Barry Tuite**
Age:	**46 years old**
Nationality:	**Australian**
Incident:	**Cassowary**
When:	**2 October 1990**
Where:	**Julatten, Queensland**
Outcome:	**Non-fatal**

Sometimes the simplest pleasures in life turn out to be more harrowing than expected. This is the unusual story of a man just minding his own business, out for a walk with his wife one afternoon near their home in northern Queensland. They expected to get some fresh air and have a bit of a chat along the way. They certainly didn't expect to be attacked by a crazed flightless bird.

Cassowary country

Barry Tuite and his wife Jenny lived in Julatten, a small township about one hour's drive from Cairns in northern Queensland. This is sugar country with vast expanses of sugar cane plantations that burn up in smoke mid-year every year. Barry worked at one of the mills. Surrounding regions grow lush tropical crops like mangoes, avocados, lychees and coffee. Julatten is a bird-watching haven, home to the wonderfully named wompoo pigeon. But that's not the only bird round here. If you drive 20 kilometres north of town, there's a settlement called Cassowary and a river of sorts by the name of Cassowary Creek. It may be sugar country, but it's cassowary country too.

One Tuesday afternoon, Barry and Jenny went for a walk along a forest road near their house. They became aware that they were being followed by a cassowary. Barry had seen two or three birds around the place before and he didn't think much of it. But this particular bird wouldn't leave them alone. It seemed to be stalking them, getting closer and closer until it was hovering over them on top of an embankment.

Barry told Jenny not to panic and he got her to walk in front of him. He picked up a stick. Suddenly there was a stomping noise, growing louder and louder. It was the cassowary trampling the ground in a display of annoyance. As Barry swung around, the bird went for him. It charged headfirst from five metres away, kicking at Barry with such force that it knocked him unconscious and sent him flying two metres across a ditch. With its dagger-like claw, the cassowary's inner toe gouged out a 12-centimetre deep hole in the left side of his chest, luckily missing his heart. It hurled itself against his rib cage, smashing through the cartilage in a terrifying attack.

Jenny ran for her life, and to seek help for her husband, across a field to her neighbour's property. The neighbour grabbed his gun and they raced back across the field together. Barry was lying, sprawled in a mass of blood, the bird still menacing him. The neighbour shot the bird dead and Barry was rushed to Cairns Base Hospital where he successfully underwent surgery. Despite the trauma, Barry's son Mark got them through with typical dry Aussie humour. 'It's safe to say that this bird had a definite attitude problem,' he said.

The colour blue

Was Barry Tuite wearing a blue shirt when he went for his walk? It's known that the colour blue can send all the wrong signals to cassowaries. Blue is of particular interest to them because it is the colour of their main food source: the blue quandong, a rich deep purple/blue fruit similar in shape and size to a large olive. A male cassowary may mistake someone wearing blue for a rival and turn aggressive. And further, when cassowaries are ready to mate, their blue feathers turn a particularly vivid blue.

It sounds callous, but, as with all animals, each attack gives researchers just a little bit more information about them. For example, four years after Barry's cassowary encounter, a jogger was chased along the road by a cassowary in northern Queensland; his only escape was to scramble up a tree. After this incident, it was found that the beat of a jogger's feet triggers aggression in the birds because it mimics the stomping noise they make when they feel under threat.

Did you know ...?

There are two recorded deaths by cassowary in Australia. In the late 1800s, a boy suspected of taunting a bird was kicked to death; and in 1926, a 17-year-old boy was killed at Mossman, about 30 kilometres north of where Barry Tuite was attacked. The story goes like this. Two brothers, Philip, 17 years old, and Granville McLean, 14 years old, lived on a farm. On this particular day they went looking for a stray horse with their hunting dog. The dog hurtled through the scrub enthusiastically and managed to startle a large adult cassowary. It seems the dog backed away but the bird went in for the kill. Granville rushed in to help but was kicked viciously in the leg. So Philip went on the offensive, which was his fatal error. He swung his horse bridle at the cassowary's head which did nothing but inflame the giant bird. It leapt into the air and lashed out at him with its razor-sharp claws. It slashed him in the neck, severing his jugular vein. With blood spurting from his throat, Philip stumbled to his feet. The two boys fled but Philip only managed to get about 200 metres before collapsing and dying.

6.
Rock

Rock is an evocative part of the imagery of Australia, from the crumbling sandstone of the Sydney basin to the awe-inspiring giant granite boulders of Karlwe Karlwe (the Devil's Marbles) in the Northern Territory. These are stories of rock: falling rock, sheer rock faces and seemingly solid but unstable rock. One is the story of a young backpacker who risks his life climbing up a waterfall; another is of a highly experienced bushwalker in the wrong place at the wrong time. But first, the story of a man who decided to walk off his jet lag and photograph the sunrise just hours after his arrival in Sydney. His first sunrise in Australia would be his last ...

CLIFF

THE MAN WHO WANTED TO PHOTOGRAPH THE SUNRISE

Name:	**Leopold Krifter**
Age:	**38 years old**
Nationality:	**Austrian**
Incident:	**Falling**
When:	**21 February 2004**
Where:	**Whale Beach, NSW**
Outcome:	**Fatal**

What makes this story so chilling is that it could happen to anyone. These two friends were at the very start of their holiday in Australia. And what they did that morning was totally unremarkable—go for a short bush walk, try to find the perfect photograph and shake off that jet lag. It just so happened that they detoured from the marked track and ended up on a cliff top that was unstable. And it just so happened that the rock collapsed underneath them, leaving one survivor and one fatality. As with many of these tales, it's easy to wonder: was this simply a tragic case of being in the wrong place at the wrong time?

Jet lag

When you fly into Sydney after the long haul from Europe, it's a relief to stand on solid ground. Air travel has the knack of leaving you fatigued and dehydrated, and once you get off the plane in a new city with a new time zone, jet lag can really kick in. One of the best antidotes is to stretch your legs, go for a walk and get some fresh air in your lungs. This was the scenario with two Austrian men who flew into Sydney for a holiday in February 2004.

They were Leopold Krifter, 38, from Steyr, an historic town in Upper Austria, and 30-year-old Mario Stangl. The pair were staying with Mario's uncle, Gerhard Zigmann, in Avalon, one of Sydney's picturesque northern beaches. Pretty soon after arrival, they decided to walk off their jet lag. So at about 6.30am, they set off for a scenic stroll and climbed a steep hill on Bangalley Headland at the southern end of Whale Beach.

There is a well-signposted walkway through the bush which warns visitors of the dangers of leaving the track. But the two men had something in mind: they wanted to find the best vantage point to take some photos of the sunrise. They left the path and walked about 15 metres to where there was a giant boulder, the perfect vantage point from which to capture the day's first light. They scrambled up onto the boulder.

Later a local resident would report that he had stood at that spot about three months earlier and decided the rock was too unstable to take his weight. Without warning, the ground under the two men shifted and the giant rock gave way. Mario fell backwards and managed to grab onto some bushes and jump free. Leopold was knocked forward by the force of the rock and toppled over the cliff.

Mario slowly opened his eyes. He sat up with a start. He was shocked but relatively unscathed, only a few scratches. But Leopold was nowhere to be seen. He looked around frantically. He yelled out into the ominous stillness, but there was no response. He ran back to his uncle's home for help. The call to Emergency Services was clocked in at 7.28am. Northern Beaches police, rescue helicopter and an ambulance team all rushed to the scene. Narrabeen paramedic Hugh Russell abseiled to the base of the cliff and searched for Leopold for more than an hour.

'Then somebody on the cliff head thought they saw a shoe so the helicopter winched me down to the rock and I found the patient underneath,' he recounted. (*The Manly Daily*, p. 1, 24 February 2004). Leopold Krifter was pinned under the giant boulder, partially buried by soil and debris, not far from the top of the cliff. His hand and foot were visible, but when the paramedic checked, there was no pulse.

A difficult rescue

All that could be done was remove the body. But this proved to be an exceedingly difficult task due to the sheer mass of the rock. Such was the weight of the boulder—estimated to weigh 8-10 tonnes—that fire brigade units were called in to help police with the excavation work. All up, it took about five hours to dislodge the rock, using a technique known as 'airbag pressure'. The body was then winched out.

Tragically, the two friends had been in Sydney for less than twelve hours. Mario's uncle, Gerhard Zigmann, thanked the Emergency Services workers, especially the policewoman who liaised with his family, praising their helpfulness and compassion. He was saddened but philosophical about the accident: 'Many people have been up there, anywhere in the world you have millions of people on similar walking tracks and just one day a stone comes loose. It's just one of those things.' (ibid, p. 2).

Mario was not coping so well. After all, he had been standing right next to Leopold one minute, and then his friend was gone. Mario would have to struggle with the haunting feelings of 'survivors' guilt', where those who have lived through trauma and seen others suffer are forced to ask, 'Why? Why wasn't it me? What could I have done?' All of them unanswerable questions.

BOULDER

THE RACE AGAINST TIME TO SURVIVE

Name:	**Warren MacDonald**
Age:	**31 years old**
Nationality:	**Australian**
Incident:	**Crushed by boulder**
When:	**Crushed 9 April; rescued 11 April 1997**
Where:	**Mount Bowen, Hinchinbrook Island, Queensland**
Outcome:	**Non-fatal**

This is an incredible story, devastating and uplifting all at once. It's about two very different men drawn together by crisis. When one of them is trapped in a life-threatening situation, they need to trust each other totally even though they have only known each other for one day. It's a race against time to survive, finding inner reserves of strength when you feel you can endure no more, keeping focus despite being physically and psychologically shot to pieces. Ultimately this is a story of dogged determination and survival with a shocking sting in the tail.

The chance meeting

They were an unlikely pair. Warren MacDonald, passionate environmentalist and bush walker from Melbourne, and Geert Van Keulen, Dutch graphic designer and sometime hiker. They met on a beach on Hinchinbrook Island at dusk. The sand was white, the light was heavenly. They sat and talked round a campfire. Geert mentioned that he wanted to climb to the top of Mount Bowen, the highest point of the island at 1142 metres. That casual conversation was the start of a terrible ordeal where both men would be stretched to their limits.

Early the next morning they headed off. It was rock-hopping rather than bush-bashing: the vegetation was so tangled that the best way up was to follow the creek bed. Geert found it hard to keep his momentum; the awkward stop and start of landing on rock after rock and choosing your trail as you went was tough. Warren found it much easier. He set the pace and found he had to slow down for Geert often. They both recognised the uneven dynamics, but neither mentioned it. After five hours of heavy going, they seemed to have gotten off course. Maybe they were in the wrong creek bed. It was getting dark so they set up camp.

After a welcome meal of tortellini, salami, melted cheese, garlic and chillies, Geert crawled into bed. Warren never made it to his sleeping bag. He went off into the darkness to 'take a leak' as he put it, climbing up the rocks on the creek edge so as not to pollute the water. All of a sudden there was a giant cracking sound and the rocks beneath him gave way. A massive granite boulder weighing more than a tonne crashed down on him, pinning him to the creek bed. He felt a sharp burning pain shoot up his body. 'F--k! Grab the torch … Mate, quick, bring the torch!' he cried out in agony (*A Test of Will*, p. 3).

Warren's left leg was completely hidden under the boulder, his right leg was visible from the knee down. Despite his predicament or perhaps because of it, he felt a certain clarity. He immediately took control of the situation, shouting out to Geert to get a small tree to act as a lever. Geert went off searching and Warren felt raindrops on his head. He was only too aware that with every minute, his situation would worsen. Alone in the dark, he willed Geert to come back.

Geert dug a suitably-sized branch in under the slab of granite and pushed with all his might. The rock moved a couple of centimetres but then the branch broke and the rock settled, as impenetrable as before. The two men looked at the broken branch with disbelief. Warren had probably broken both his legs. How the hell would they get him out? And the rain kept falling.

Geert rummaged around for his Swiss Army knife. Frantically he started slashing away at a bigger tree, cutting himself on the palm of his hand in the process. His glasses were foggy and smeared with rain. The creek bed was beginning to rise until it was almost at Warren's waist. Which raised a further question of survival: would he drown before they managed to pull him free?

Then began a frenzy of activity, hacking trees—how Geert wished they had a decent axe—levering the rock, the tree snapping. Of course, any tree that could be hacked off with a Swiss Army knife wasn't strong enough to lever a gigantic boulder. They both knew that. But they had to keep trying. One final attempt. The tree cracked with a horrible sound signifying defeat, hopelessness and something worse. Fear.

Warren was a tough-minded individual, who had trained himself all his life to be self-reliant and to push the boundaries of his comfort zone. But now he found himself so vulnerable, unable to move and totally reliant on a less experienced bush walker. He let out a soft groan.

And then the rain stopped. Geert sat down next to Warren and put his arm around him. There was nothing to say.

Eight hours gone

4am. Warren had been trapped for eight hours, sitting in cold water, no feeling in his mutilated legs. Geert must walk out and get help; down the mountain to the ferry. But there was only one ferry a day, so if he missed it …

Both of them had thought long and hard about Geert's journey. It was a long way down. Last night's downpour had flooded the creek bed which meant he would have to cut his way down through the thick rainforest; exactly what they had deliberately avoided on the way up. Geert was not the most experienced of bush walkers and they both knew it. This was one of the most emotionally gruelling points of their brief relationship. Geert knew that Warren's survival was in his hands. And Warren knew that when Geert left, he would be alone.

They talked about the fact that Warren would be alone for at least one more night, and then it was time for Geert to leave. He left Warren with three plastic bags attached to a cord with some odds and ends: dried fruit, some bread and cheese, a mug, a torch, an extra shirt, some socks to wear as gloves, his notebook and pen. Only later did Warren realise the implications of this last item: perhaps Geert meant him to write down his dying thoughts.

Geert's first hundred metres were not encouraging, more cartoonish than real-life drama. He slipped in the creek almost immediately, picked himself up and hurried on. He had to make his own path, slashing through the undergrowth. The vegetation scratched at him with sharp needle-like leaves and the more he hurried, the more he stumbled. He had to remind himself again and again to stay calm. He was no use to Warren in a state of panic.

Going up was hard enough, but the descent was ten times worse. He had two poor choices: struggle through dense undergrowth or tackle slippery rocks and waterfalls. He had to fight the instinct to go as quickly as possible; a twisted ankle would make everything a thousand times worse.

Geert slipped into chest-deep water, carefully feeling his way along the rocks. He was attacked by a nest of green ants, agonising, biting him under his raincoat and t-shirt. He tossed off his rucksack and jumped into the creek, frantically flicking them off to stop the pain. And all the while there was the maddening sound of the bush: a million insects, the cries of a thousand birds. It wasn't a peaceful place, it was a cacophony of sound and to someone who avoided the noise of the city it was maddening. 'Yet it was useful,' Geert would later write, 'It kept me awake and on edge.' (ibid, p. 65).

Hour after hour, Warren's mind was a rush of memories, fears, fantasies and events from his past that had given him strength. At 6pm, heavy rain began again, crashing down on his immobile semi-reclined figure. His thoughts ebbed in and out, sometimes positive, sometimes the depths of despair. His mind started playing tricks on him, hallucinating, dreaming, tossing between wake and sleep. 'This is it mate, this is your ultimate test,' he thought to himself (ibid, p. 42). He felt nauseous, hypothermic and sick, so sick. He wondered whether he would be strong enough to pull through. The possibility that he wouldn't was the thing that terrified him. And there was nothing but night.

Geert was awake, ready to keep walking. He had been walking already for 20 hours and was starting to lose it. He was exhausted, overwhelmed by the enormity of his task. He couldn't do it and he didn't care. He needed to find some inner reserve to keep going. He sat down to empty his boots and almost burst into tears: he was wearing Warren's purple socks. That was all he needed to spur him on.

The water was turning red. There was a freshwater crayfish eating Warren's foot but he couldn't feel a thing. He scared it away with a stick, wondering whether he would lose his foot. It was so cold. He was drifting in and out of consciousness. Ants marched across him, lining up to feast on his rotting flesh. He had been trapped for 35 hours. And for 25 of those hours, he had been alone with his thoughts.

Contact

Geert reached the base of Mount Bowen and then the ocean. He retched and kept going. And then he saw two figures in the distance, hikers from Queensland waiting for the ferry back to Cardwell. He rushed at them, babbling like a madman. The words came out with difficulty. His mouth was dry, his tongue like lead. One of them went back to look out for the ferry, the other went with him to the beach. The ferry was supposed to arrive at noon. But it didn't come. Would it come? They built a fire, throwing in paper and plastic washed up on the beach to make thick black smoke. The hiker got a stick and wrote in the sand in letters a metre high: SOS. MAN TRAPPED UNDER ROCK FOR 36 HOURS.

Finally, after an eternity, the ferry arrived. Goody, the trusty captain, took Geert on board and sped out through the mangroves to find somewhere with decent transmission to send a mayday. But his radio wouldn't work. So they headed out further to where the crab boats were, where they found an old salt who managed—after several attempts—to get though to Hinchinbrook Resort on a nearby island. The ferry dropped Geert back on the island and left with the hikers. It was 2.30pm. Geert sat on the beach, gazing back at Mount Bowen. He couldn't take his eyes off it.

By late afternoon, Warren had given up. 'So this is what it's like to die slowly, all alone, out in the bush. It doesn't feel as glamorous as I thought it would …' (ibid, p. 74). Then he heard the sweetest sound: the sound of helicopter blades. He grabbed his tarp and waved it wildly. The chopper was almost directly over him then it turned back towards the coast. The next five to ten minutes were agonising as he waited for it to return. The chopper reappeared. It tilted forward and swooped in a wide circle. Warren could see someone at the window. It circled once more before disappearing again. They'd seen him.

The rescue operation

The rescue was extremely precarious. Another half-hour longer and they would have needed to pull out for the night. The medical team was winched in. Warren was given an IV drip with morphine and anti-nausea medication, followed by saline and Hartmans solution to raise his blood pressure and minimise risk of kidney failure when the rock was lifted. Then began a torturous two-and-a-half hour operation.

The critical point was when the rock shifted, because at that moment the toxins and potassium that had built up in his legs would rush back into his bloodstream and he could die. It all came to a head: the morphine, the shock, the nausea, the anguish. In the state he was in, Warren became obsessed with the idea of the rock falling on him again. The doctor gave him a shot of adrenalin and they were ready. Warren was airlifted to Cairns Base Hospital in critical condition with a crushed pelvis and two broken legs. His legs were so badly damaged that they were both amputated above the knee.

10 January 1998, nine months after the accident. Geert Van Keulen is living in Adelaide, still coming to terms with his part in the whole episode. Warren MacDonald is still the same thoughtful, determined, fit, driven man as before, it's just that now where his legs used to be, there is

nothing. He works at rehabilitation, strengthening his arms, building up his endurance, becoming capable. His first major goal is The Pier to Pub, a 1.2 kilometre swim at Lorne, two hours west of Melbourne. He crosses the finish line in 23 minutes and 1 second, leaving 259 competitors to come to grips with the fact that they have been beaten by a man with no legs (ibid, p.173). Since then, Warren has continued to do awesome things to challenge himself, climbing to the top of Cradle Mountain in Tasmania and hitting the summit of Mt Kilamanjaro, the highest mountain in Africa. But that's another story.

WATERFALL

THE BACKPACKER AND THE AVOIDABLE DEATH

Name:	**Jeroen Adriaan van der Zwaan**
Age:	**19 years old**
Nationality:	**Dutch**
Incident:	**Falling**
When:	**20 January 2003**
Where:	**Murray Falls near Tully, Queensland.**
Outcome:	**Fatal**

Some tragedies are unforeseen and shocking in their randomness. Others—in hindsight or even at the time—are avoidable. This is one such death. It's the sorry story of a young Dutch tourist who decides to go exploring on top of a waterfall in North Queensland. But to do so, he has to climb over the carefully positioned guard rails and head away from the designated tracks which have been put there for a purpose. Sometimes you can get away with a bit of bush whacking on the edge of a sheer rock face, but in this case, the young man doesn't live to enjoy the view. His death is tragic, senseless and avoidable. If only he had stuck to the path.

Respect for the land

Murray Falls is a sacred area for the local Aboriginal people and a traditional hunting, fishing and swimming area. The Chair of the Jumbun community, Marcia Jerry, has said, 'It is not a place of fear for us, because we were always taught to observe traditional rules and how to treat the place with respect.' (*Cairns Post*, p. 5, 22 January 2003). Respect for the landscape, caution in unfamiliar places and awe for unique natural beauty are things of great value. But sometimes they get lost in the excitement of travel, the desire to push your limits, that rush of adrenalin when you see an irresistible challenge …

Jeroen van der Zwaan was a 19-year-old student from the district of Sassenheim in The Netherlands. He had been backpacking around Australia with his mate, Bart Vandermeij. On 19 January 2003, they camped at Mission Beach, about one-and-a-half hours' drive south of Cairns, on the Great Barrier Reef. The next day they went with some friends to see Murray Falls, a popular tourist attraction of scenic cascades and granite pools about 40 kilometres south of Tully.

The top of the falls is quite treacherous and off-limits to the public. But Jeroen went bush, off the designated track into the area above the falls. To do this, he had to climb over guardrails and ignore signposted walking tracks. He plunged to his death at about 1pm.

Twenty-metre fall

He fell more than 20 metres, smashing onto the rocks on the way down and plummetting into the pool below. His friends dragged him from the waterhole severely injured and tried to resuscitate him. He was rushed to Tully Hospital but died soon after arrival.

Police described the tragedy as 'avoidable'. 'These tragedies can be avoided if people use commonsense and stick to the designated route,' said Innisfail Police District Inspector Paul Taylor in response to the incident (ABC newsonline, abc.net.au 22 January 2003). Several tourists had died at the falls in recent years and, as a result, the Queensland Parks and Wildlife Service had installed many signs and guardrails with clearly marked walking tracks in an attempt to keep people safe. 'These falls do have a history and there have been a number of incidents at what is a very beautiful spot ... national parks have gone to great lengths to ensure there is a safe route for people to take in the scenery but, unfortunately, people do not always stay on the path,' he said. (*Cairns Post*, p. 1, 21 January 2003).

Jeroen's friend Bart collected his belongings from Tully and flew back to the Netherlands the very next day.

Did you know ...?

Is it dangerous to be Dutch? Off the record, Jeroen Adriaan van der Zwaan was the fourteenth Dutch tourist to die in Australia over a 12-month period. Further, he was the third Dutch tourist to be involved in a serious incident in Far North Queensland within one month. First, there was Lienne Schellekens, the 18-year-old Dutch tourist attacked by a hammerhead shark off Upolu Cay near Cairns on 29 December 2002 (See 'The Hammerhead that Lunged at Lienne', chapter 1).

Then there was Jan-Paul Swagemakers, the 25-year-old Dutch man who died while snorkelling at Saxby Reef off Cairns less than two weeks later on 9 January 2003. In another bizarre connection to the story, Jeroen was the second person in less than three weeks to die from falling off a waterfall in Far North Queensland. His untimely death followed the death of a 29-year-old Mackay man who slipped on a rock and fell to his death at Roaring Meg Falls near Cooktown on New Year's Eve.

7.
Mountain

Mountains in Australia take on many shapes and forms. There are the dry dusty mountains of iron ore to the north-west and the rugged beauty of Tasmania's wilderness areas. Then there are the snowfields of the Victorian Alps and the Snowy Mountains, where these stories are set. There's the happy-ending tale of a young woman lost in rugged terrain for four days; and the story of four young snowboarders who die in the shelter of their snow cave. But first, Australia's worst landslide when 18 people died, a story made all the more poignant by the survival of just one man.

LANDSLIDE

Since written records began in 1842, there have been more than 90 deaths from landslides in Australia. In 1928, six men were killed when a railway embankment between Blackwood and Belair in South Australia collapsed, thought to be brought on by heavy rain and traffic vibrations. In 1996, a 14-metre high limestone cliff collapsed on spectators sheltering from the rain at a school surf carnival at Cowaramup Bay near Gracetown, Margaret River, in Western Australia. 2500 tonnes of sand and rock rained down, killing five adults and four children. Four people died and fourteen were injured near the Visitors' Centre in Cradle Mountain National Park, Tasmania in 2001 when the shoulder of Dove Lake Road gave way, sending a bus plunging down into a ravine. But the worst landslide—in terms of fatalities—and certainly the most well-known is Thredbo, 1997.

THREDBO: EIGHTEEN DEAD AND ONE ALIVE

Name:	**Stuart Diver**
Age:	**27 years old**
Nationality:	**Australian**
Incident:	**Landslide**
When:	**Buried under debris 30 July 1997; rescued 2 August 1997**
Where:	**Thredbo, Snowy Mountains, NSW**
Outcome:	**Non-fatal**

To most Australians, the Thredbo landslide is a tragedy with a miraculous ending. After nearly 66 hours and the discovery of 18 bodies, one man was found alive: Stuart Diver. Diver's astonishing survival eclipsed the deaths of the other victims, coming at a time when hope had all but run out. Press releases, rescue officials and newspaper reports bluntly hinted that no-one could realistically still be alive after two nights of sub-zero temperatures. But Diver made it. And his painstaking rescue, captured all the way on national television, was an amazing study in human endurance and the will to live; as well as the innate human drive to find, sustain and save.

Diver's rescue was a celebration of life. But painted against a backdrop of so many deaths, it would always be tinged with sadness. And that's what Thredbo is. Joy and mourning, despair mixed with relief, the cruelty of death versus the extraordinary power of survival.

Voices from the rubble

It started with a leaking water main. Water saturated a large section of the embankment below the Alpine Way, the road that cuts its way above Thredbo Village from Jindabyne to the Victorian border. Late one Wednesday night in July 1997, part of the slope collapsed without warning. There was a blast like an explosion, a roar like a terrible wind and the smell of petrol fumes. 1000 tonnes of earth, rock and trees plummeted down the slope, crashing into Carinya Lodge 100 metres below.

The sheer force pushed Carinya off its foundations and across Bobuck Lane where it went smashing into another lodge, Bimbadeen. A woman who happened to be walking along the lane was swept away. An ugly 100-metre gash scarred the landscape. All that was left was one lodge roof flattened on the snow and the other lodge roof up on its side resting against a tree. That solitary gum tree stopped the landslide going any further. It was all over in 10 seconds.

But it wasn't over at all. Lights flickered and went out. There was pitch black. And silence. Then car alarms began to pierce the ominous calm. A fire siren squealed out into the black. And a peaceful winter's night exploded into chaos.

Immediately afterwards, voices arose from the rubble. A political reporter on holiday in Thredbo heard three weak voices. A ski instructor and a paramedic both heard screaming, and more unnervingly, they recognised the voices. They were the voices of a US couple, Mike and Mariam 'Mim' Sodergren, two highly regarded ski instructors who spent their northern winters in USA and their southern winters in Thredbo. The ski instructor started digging frantically through the concrete and bricks to reach the voices. He found a ski manual inscribed 'M. Sodergren' and knew for certain that it was Mike Sodergren who he could hear crying out in pain.

The paramedic, who pushed through police lines to get to the scene, called out, 'Mike, it's Davo, can you hear me?' but Sodergren didn't respond. He just kept crying out, 'Don't let me die, don't let me die'. Both men also recognised the strangely calm voice of Mike's wife, Mim. 'Is that you, Mim?' they asked but all they got back was an eerie 'hello' over and over again as if the entrapped had entered another world. They couldn't hear anyone above but they were crying their hearts out anyway.

Five minutes after the landslide, the Thredbo Fire Brigade arrived and ordered everyone off site, fearing another landslide. The ski instructor asked a policeman if he was going to stay with the Sodergrens. The officer said he would, but he didn't; the ski instructor saw him walk away. At the inquest, this exact issue was raised. How distressing it was to know there were people crying for help minutes after the event, trapped under the ground, people you knew personally, but no one could help them. Wouldn't you go in there with your bare hands? Wouldn't you scream and fight and not take an official 'no' for an answer? The coordinator of the rescue, Sergeant Garry Smith, is on record as saying that the area where the Sodergrens' voices were heard was not searched because it was 'very difficult to get there'.

The first police arrived at 12:20am and evacuated neighbouring lodges, turning Thredbo Alpine Resort into a makeshift evacuation centre. At 1.30am, police decided it was too dangerous to attempt further rescues and called for expert assessment.

The temperature dropped to -10°C. Various NSW Fire Brigade units, ambulances and State Emergency Services began to arrive, but were hampered by fog around Cooma and crowded conditions in Thredbo car

SEE AUSTRALIA AND DIE

park. Tow trucks were called in to get inessential cars out of the way.

At dawn it was 2°C and fine. Locals gathered in shock to look across the valley to where two lodges used to be: a scene of utter devastation under a light powdering of snow. Hundreds of emergency service workers continued to arrive from near and far. Water was still gushing from the burst water main. Major emergency services secured broken water, gas and oil lines as well as dealing with dangerously unstable boulders and concrete slabs. Engineers started to build a reinforced road adjacent to the affected area to allow heavy machinery on site. Four trees in the way of rescue efforts were removed. A roadblock was set up 15 kilometres from the scene. A geophysicist from Sydney was called in to assess risk of further collapse. Special Medivac fixed wing aircraft were flown in from Sydney as freezing temperatures and ice in the air made it impossible for rescue helicopters to land.

Agonising delay

It was all systems go. Except where it mattered, on site. The lack of action, the time ticking by with nothing to show for it, caused massive distress for friends and relatives waiting. Everyone in Thredbo knew someone buried under the rubble and the delay was agonising. Thredbo employees yelled and screamed at police. Some were forcibly restrained as they pushed against police lines, desperate to get to their trapped colleagues and at least do something. Rescue workers primed to go found themselves waiting hour after hour. But the decision had been made that nothing would be done until Robin Fell—Department of Geotechnical Engineering, University of NSW—had assessed the safety risk. It's alleged police took eight hours to contact him. Certainly he did not arrive at Thredbo until 10am. Whatever the story, Fell gave the go-ahead for careful preliminary removal of rubble at 10.30am on Thursday morning.

A cautious rescue effort began. The first rescuers worked their way across the site, secured by safety harnesses and ropes. At 11am, a backhoe started digging towards the main lodge so rescuers could tunnel towards any survivors. At noon, the coordinator called for total silence on site so that any muted cries for help could be heard. The rescue teams, including friends and relatives of the missing, formed human chains and gingerly began to spread out across the rubble. At 2pm, firemen started digging a path towards the centre of the site. In a risky operation, a rescue worker was lowered by police helicopter to search cars among the debris for possible survivors. There were none. The day's progress wasn't aided by several minor landslides.

By mid-afternoon the site was abuzz with activity. Seismic detectors that could register a heartbeat or even a finger moving were placed in the rubble. Rescuers called, 'If you can hear us, move your fingers.' But there was no movement from beneath. Slim tubes with speaker-microphones were inserted into the rubble. Miniature fibre-optic 'lipstick' cameras which give a 360-degree view were sent four metres under the surface. Thermal imaging cameras which could detect body heat scoured the area. But there were no signs of life. Specialist urban rescue teams dubbed 'the tunnel rats' pushed under concrete, trees, mangled metal and mud. There were serious difficulties cutting the concrete slabs because the chainsaws were lubricated by water and, in sub-zero temperatures, the water froze. And all throughout the day, police turned away the families of those missing.

That evening, Superintendent Charlie Sanderson, Monaro Local Area Commander, fronted up to the Thredbo Alpine Hotel bistro and met an overwhelming crowd of 600. He felt the bitterness in the air. He justified the delayed start of the rescue operation: 'You may think we've made the wrong decisions ... there will be a thorough investigation later,' he explained. 'The risk of future catastrophe and of injuring or killing our own people had to be weighed against the sensible way of tackling the problem. We are all devastated with what's happened. I can't tell you how sorry I am for you all.' (*Herald-Sun*, p. 3, 1 August 1997). And sadly, after less than 24 hours, he conceded that the chance of finding anyone alive was 'very, very negligible.'

An hour later, the first body was found, that of John Cameron from

Sydney, the only occupant of Carinya Lodge that night. He had died instantly of suffocation.

More subzero temperatures. Under floodlights, rescuers gave their all as they worked through the night, trying to find survivors, at times resorting to using their bare hands. The NSW Police Chief Superintendent described the chances of finding survivors as 'ever diminishing'.

A new day dawned. Over 400 personnel were now involved in the rescue operation. The second body had been found. Expensive diamond-tipped chainsaws were brought in to tackle the concrete slabs in the hope that someone might have survived between the cavities. Another dismal assessment: Superintendent Charlie Sanderson rated the chance of finding survivors 'infinitesimally small'.

Saturday's miracle

The first glimmer of hope shone out in the frosty pre-dawn light. A chainsaw was grinding away. Ambulance service rescue workers were using sound detection equipment under a concrete slab. Steve Hirst, a firefighter with expertise in structural collapse, thought he heard muffled sounds. After calling for silence, he lay down on his stomach and yelled, 'Rescue team working overhead—can anyone hear me?' There was a murmur. He repeated the cry. The words came back, 'I can hear you'. It was 5.37am. The voice belonged to Stuart Diver.

The 12-hour rescue effort that followed was covered live on national television. Rescuers dug a 10-centimetre hole through the final two metres of rubble to reach the cavity where Stuart Diver was trapped. He was lying on his back, entombed in concrete.

Dr Richard Morris, an intensive-care specialist, spent the day in the cavity above him. Through a hole the size of a fist, he inserted a drip into Stuart's foot. While he nurtured Stuart's physical well-being, Paul Featherstone, a paramedic, stuck with him the whole day too, nurturing his psychological health. 'We talked about the snow on a nice sunny, crisp, clear day,' Featherstone said. He promised Stuart that he'd be out by afternoon and they'd have a look at it together.

He wasn't far wrong. Just before 5.30pm, Stuart Diver was lifted out of his concrete tomb on a stretcher to shouts of 'Good on you, Stewie!', 'Go, Stewie!' and wild cheers. First to his side was his brother Euan, one of the first volunteers to respond to the disaster alert. That day, Steve Hirst, who first heard the muffled sounds below, earned a new nickname, 'The Man with the Bionic Ear'.

Stuart Diver had been on his back for nearly 66 hours in pitch black, not knowing day from night. He had no idea how long he had been there. The concrete slab overhead was only centimetres from his face. Several times he had nearly drowned but managed to keep his nose above water. His wife Sally had been beside him. Every time the water rose around them, he had stretched out to raise her head above water-level, believing her to be alive and unconscious. But she was dead.

As he emerged from his tomb, the dusky light hit his beloved Thredbo Valley. He looked at his paramedic companion who had lived through the entire day with him. And in a croaky voice, Stuart Diver said, 'That sky's fantastic.'

Did you know?

A memorial now stands on site at Thredbo. It is a simple structure of timber, with eighteen columns signifying the eighteen lives lost. The names of the dead are:

- Dianne Elizabeth Ainsworth, Housekeeper, Thredbo Alpine Hotel
- John Anthony Cameron, 46 years old, Carpenter from Drummoyne, Sydney
- Barry Achim Decker, Accountant
- Sally Sophia Diver, Receptionist, Thredbo Alpine Hotel
- Diane Lee Hoffman, Head Housekeeper, Thredbo Alpine Hotel
- Werner Jecklin, Ski Slopes Manager
- Oskar Walter Luhn, Maintenance Chairlift Worker
- Andrew Stuart McArthur, Maintenance Worker
- Stephen Thomas Moss, c30 years old, Catering Manager
- Wendy Anne O`Donoghue, mid-30's, Marketing Manager, Thredbo Alpine Village
- Mary Frances Phillips, 31 years old, NZ Ski Instructor
- Aino Valgamae Senbruns, partner of Oscar Luhn
- Mariam Alice Sodergren, 41 years old, US Ski Instructor
- Michael Lee Sodergren, 46 years old, US Ski Instructor
- Steven Urosevic, 32 years old, Front Office Manager at Thredbo Alpine Hotel.
- Colin John Warren, 40's, Property Manager with Kosciuszko-Thredbo Company.
- David Glenn Watson, 30's, Bistro Supervisor at Cascades Restaurant
- Anthony John Weaver, 47 years old, Head of Thredbo Ski Patrol

LOST

SURVIVING THE SNOWY MOUNTAINS

Name:	**Zuzana Stevichova**
Age:	**23 years old**
Nationality:	**Czech**
Incident:	**Lost**
When:	**Reported missing 16 December 2003; found 20 December 2003**
Where:	**Jacobs River, Snowy Mountains, NSW**
Outcome:	**Non-fatal**

This is a remarkable survival story. Not just because a young Czech woman survived four nights lost in Kosciuszko National Park but because of the intensive search and rescue operation. To give you some idea of the logistics involved in looking for one missing bushwalker, there were 35–50 personnel out looking for her every day for four days until she was found. They covered over 100 square kilometres in an aerial search and 10 square kilometres on the ground in difficult terrain and terrible weather conditions. Federal and State police, sniffer dogs, horses, helicopters, emergency services, fire brigades and volunteers; you name it, they all converged on the Jacobs River region near Thredbo to find her. Many stories like this end in tragedy but, happily, this one doesn't.

Out for a hike

Zuzana Stevichova set out from Dead Horse Gap in the Snowy Mountains with her sister, Eva, her brother-in-law, Ondrej and their friend, Van, on Tuesday 16 December 2003 at about 12.30pm. They were going to walk to The Chimneys, at 1885 metres the highest point in the area. This was brumby country. In fact, Dead Horse Gap is so-called because of the wild horses that sometimes become trapped there during blinding snowstorms.

It was a three-hour, 16-kilometre round trip. By the time the group reached the base, Zuzana was feeling tired. So, leaving her back-pack with her sister, she turned back, saying she'd meet them back at the car. Later, when the other three returned to the car, she wasn't there. They retraced their steps back to The Chimneys but they couldn't find her.

Eva alerted police at 8.30 that night and a preliminary search of the area was carried out. A full-scale search was organised for the next day.

The next day a large-scale search operation got underway. NSW Police, the Pol Air police helicopter, NSW National Parks and Wildlife Service, Thredbo Fire Brigade and Emergency Service volunteers scoured the area. It was hoped the weather would stay fine because Zuzana wasn't prepared for overnight hiking. She was only wearing light summer clothes, a t-shirt and shorts. She had a hat and some sunglasses but no food or water.

There were concerns about her health. She needed medication for epilepsy three times a day, but she wasn't carrying any tablets. Despite this, rescuers were hopeful that she was alive. Perhaps she had fallen and sprained her ankle or perhaps she had got lost. The overnight temperatures had been mild—only going down to about 10°C—and if she stuck close to the river, there would be plenty of water. The search continued until 4.30pm.

On Day Two of the search, Pol Air continued an aerial search of creeks and rivers. The ground search was expanded to about 50 personnel. About 35 police officers using tracker dogs searched along Jacobs River, near an old tin mine fire trail. They were supported by the Snowy Mountains Horse Riders' Association, as well as Jindabyne and Cooma SES. Bushfires had been through the area so it was fairly open country but there were swampy patches. A 100 square kilometre aerial search and a 10 square kilometre ground search failed to find any trace of her.

On Day Three, the Federal Police Search and Rescue Team joined the search. Finally, that afternoon there was good news. At about 2pm, searchers made a positive discovery: a footprint matching her shoe size.

It was near Tea Tree Creek, to the south-west of where Zuzana was last seen.

Eight more footprints were found a couple of hours later. Two teams of searchers immediately concentrated their search in the Tea Tree Creek area. But conditions turned nasty. Dense fog and cloud cover restricted visibility severely while heavy rain made the tracks impassable. The terrain was so difficult and the weather so bad that they had to winch the teams out and leave the vehicles in. Before suspending the search for the night, they set up an observation post between the Tin Mine Fire Trail and Jacobs River.

They also set up some spotlights, angling them to shine down the river, which would give Zuzana some guidance if she wanted to cover any distance during the night. At least the rescuers were honing in on the lost walker. Tomorrow was sure to bring good results.

Day Four: zeroing in

Saturday. The search area was carefully mapped out. Searchers were given their target area and specific grid references. Because the area was so rugged, planes dropped the teams into specific areas. Soon more encouraging signs were found: more footprints, broken branches and flattened grass which looked as though Zuzana had slept there during the night. At last, at midday, there was a positive sighting. She was spotted sitting on the banks of Jacobs River, about nine kilometres from where she was last seen. After four nights lost in the Snowy, Zuzana Stevichova was finally safe. And she was deliriously happy.

A paramedic was winched in to treat her for dehydration and hypothermia. She was given her medication and a warm Sustagen drink. Given her five–day, four-night ordeal, she was in pretty good shape. Eva was thrilled to be reunited with her intrepid-explorer-sister, praising the rescue teams and expressing her gratitude for the scale of the rescue operation: 'It's so amazing how the police worked here for so long a time. We almost gave up, but they didn't—it's so nice. Thank you!'

Zuzana was airlifted to Cooma Hospital by the Snowy Hydro Southcare helicopter. Commander of the Police Search Team, Russell Eastham, described her survival as remarkable, saying that they were 'getting to the stage that the possibility of not having a happy ending was more likely than not'.

It had been a challenging search and rescue. Difficult weather conditions, rugged terrain and the need to winch search teams into the area had added an extra degree of difficulty to the entire operation. Indeed, without the combined expertise of dozens of emergency and rescue workers, the story could have had a very different ending. So it's rather an understatement when Acting Inspector Kim Taylor of Thredbo Police Station summed up the final rescue with a hint of modesty, 'I'd say it's been a very hard day …'

As for Zuzana, she was transferred to Canberra Hospital and discharged the same night. The two sisters left Australia on Christmas Eve to fly home for a joyful and very memorable white Christmas.

SUFFOCATION

THE SNOWBOARDERS AND THE SNOW CAVE

Name:	**Scott Beardsmore**
Age:	**26 years old**
Name:	**Paul Beardsmore**
Age:	**24 years old**
Name:	**Timothy Friend**
Age:	**25 years old**
Name:	**Dean Pincini**
Age:	**25 years old**
Nationality:	**Australian**
Incident:	**Accidental Suffocation**
When:	**16 November 1999**
Where:	**Thredbo, Snowy Mountains, NSW**
Outcome:	**Fatal**

Imagine four young snowboarders, all in their mid-20s with their lives ahead of them. They are competent, motivated and well-equipped for outdoor adventure. Their friends and families are certain that whatever happens, they will get through it and come out alive. Youth and physical fitness are a strong combination, but in this story it isn't enough. Nature is stronger. One fateful day in August 1999, the four friends catch the Thredbo chairlift up to Mount Crackenback. The weather is abysmal and the blizzard conditions continue for the next three days. Experienced skiers turn back that day, but the four press on, regardless.

Great mates

Dean Pincini, Timothy Friend and Scott Beardsmore were mates from way back. Paul was Scott's younger brother. They'd gone to school together in French's Forest, a northern suburb of Sydney. Their parents had encouraged them to be fit, active and resourceful and they were a foursome who lived life to the fullest. Canyoning, indoor rock climbing … Dean had even built rock climbing walls in his garage! Their snowboarding trips to Thredbo were an almost annual pilgrimage. They started making plans for their three-day adventure in Thredbo.

Two days before the trip, equipment was everywhere: GPS, thermal clothes, snowboarding boots, sleeping bags, torches and snow shovels as well as supplies like dried noodles, chocolate bars and energy drinks. They pored over maps and selected a spot about 10 kilometres from the Thredbo chairlift between Lake Albina and Racecourse Gully. That was where they would build their snow cave. They left detailed plans of their proposed route with families and friends and then headed for the Snowy Mountains.

Saturday morning. The four mates picked up their hired snow poles from Rebel Sports at Perisher. The staff there warned them about the weather. But when they got on the chairlift at Thredbo, the weather was fine. Paul rang his dad at about 9.20am and told him they were just heading off.

The early morning forecast was for deteriorating conditions on Sunday night. But the bad weather came in much earlier than predicted. Just before 10am, the snow started blowing in. It was getting towards white-out conditions on the Main Range and visibility was down to 100 metres.

Last sightings

At the top of the chairlift, a ski patroller who'd just done his check of the ski runs noticed the four snowboarders. A waiter looking out the window of Eagles Nest restaurant saw the four young men too. He was probably the last person to see them alive. It was 10.30am.

On the mountains that day, experienced hikers turned back. But the foursome pushed on, following the poles of the Lakes Walk towards Mount Kosciuszko. They were walking into a strong head wind and they did not have snowshoes. Conditions were so difficult that two kilometres was all they could manage. They stopped and set up camp for the night to wait out the storm.

Dean, the most experienced of the four, had learned the finer points of snow cave design in Canada. He had read up on them, could sketch accurate designs and had run through overnight survival techniques.

They chose a spot about 500 metres from the track to build their snow cave. It wasn't snowing as they started to dig. A photo remains, showing them in their prime. Working together, smiling, snow shovels in hand.

Outside was 0°C. Inside was warm and protected. They crawled into the snow cave, leaving their ski poles outside, resting upright against the wall near the entrance. They had candles and torches for light. They cooked a meal using one of two gas stoves they'd brought. And then they settled down to sleep.

That night there was an unusually heavy snow dump. And a portentous event. About one kilometre away, a group of scouts had built a snow cave too. One of the adult leaders was camped solo nearby. During the night, he awoke to find his tent being buried in snow; the scouts' snow cave was well on its way to being buried too. He dug them out and kept vigil for the rest of the night.

Outside Dean, Tim, Scott and Paul's snow cave, snow was slowly beginning to seal up the entrance. The depth of snowfall was not crucial, it was the amount of snow being blown across the ground with such force that was the deciding factor. No matter how well-designed and no matter what size or shape, any cave would have been buried by snow that night. A vent to the outside was essential, not so much for allowing oxygen in, but for allowing carbon dioxide to get out. It is possible to breathe through a snow wall for some hours but only if there is no build-up of carbon dioxide. A vent to the outside is the difference between life and death.

Veteran skiers said it was the worst weather they'd ever seen. And it continued. Sunday passed. And Monday.

The deadline passes

'If you don't hear from me by 8pm on Monday, then worry,' were Dean's parting words to his family. Ten minutes after the Monday deadline passed, relatives contacted Jindabyne police. Police found their car in the car park at Thredbo, their mobile phones inside. But no sign of the four young men.

7.am Tuesday 10 August. Seamans Hut was set up as the forward command post and a full search commenced, headed by Sergeant Warren Denham who had been at the scene of the Thredbo landslide in 1997 (See 'Thredbo: Eighteen Dead and One Alive', this chapter). From that, he had learnt that even when it looks like there's no way in the world someone could survive, you cannot give up.

It was one of the largest searches ever in the Snowy Mountains and was undertaken in the worst conditions Sgt Denham had seen in over seven years. Priority one wind gale warnings, winds up to 110 kilometres per hour and white-out conditions hindered the search with frustrating regularity. Searchers had to continually reassess their own safety and the search was stopped and restarted several times.

During the first week, beacons and food parcels were left at three different locations near Seaman's Hut. Thirty-five police, National Parks rangers and sniffer dogs searched the area. Other searchers were out on cross-country skis and snow mobiles. The most likely places were searched and re-searched. Nothing.

13 August. The search area was expanded to the Thredbo River between Perisher and Guthega in case the four had decided to go around the mountains. The weather was still against the searchers. A planned explosion to remove ice hanging over a snowslide where the four might be trapped was abandoned due to high winds.

Optimism still reigned. Alpine experts believed that even after one week, survival was still possible. The parents of the four young men told reporters they were confident their sons were alive. Relatives, their old high school principal and the French's Forest community echoed their sentiments. The boys were competent, fit and resourceful: they would get through.

15 August. Finally, a day of near perfect conditions allowed for the use of thermal imaging equipment. Three helicopters searched the scrub below the Main Range with heat-seeking devices but the bush was so thick that searchers had to be winched in to check heat sources. The following night, an Army plane flew over with thermal imaging equipment. But there were no positive sightings.

Scaling down the search

18 August. Nine days had gone by. Over 200 local and interstate police, firefighters, State Emergency Service workers and other volunteers were involved. The 300 square kilometre search area had been covered twice and, in some places, three times. The search was to be scaled down to 20 people and a helicopter.

The next day, there was a short-lived glimmer of hope. Thermal imaging photos showed a so-called 'hot spot' thought to be a human form sheltering under a rock. Search teams spent most of the day pinpointing the location, but it turned out to be a dead wallaby.

The following day brought howling weather back again. White-out conditions and 130 kilometre per hour winds brought the search to a standstill. Only a miracle could save them now.

The families of the missing snowboarders were in a state of numbness, fading optimism coupled with a sense of dread. How could four young men disappear? Who could know what the parents and the searchers were thinking and feeling? The helplessness, the anxiety, the uncertainty.

After twenty fruitless days, police faced the inevitable. The four missing men were most likely buried under the snow and wouldn't be found until the snow melted. The search was called off on 29 August.

Over September and October, there were sporadic search attempts—

both unofficial and official—but they were hampered by freak snow dumps and gale force winds.

By the end of spring, much of the snow had melted. A new search began on 15 November with RAN helicopter teams, Federal and State Police Search and Rescue. This search was scheduled to last for four days, but that proved to be unnecessarily optimistic.

The next day, the naval helicopter HMAS *Albatross* was flying over the Main Range when the pilot saw a black hole in the side of a snowdrift, one of the few patches of snow still remaining. It was 2.2 kilometres south of Seamans Hut and less than three kilometres from the top of the Crackenback chair lift where the four had started out all those weeks before.

The pilot landed and went to investigate. What he found was ski poles sticking out of the snow. And a body in the entrance of the snow cave. Search teams had passed over this very site several times early in the search but it had been too deeply buried.

Cause of death

The deaths of Dean Pincini, Timothy Friend, Scott Beardsmore and Paul Beardsmore were determined to be as a result of 'accidental suffocation' with 'possible hypothermia' (two victims), 'consistent with hypothermia' and 'combined effects of hypothermia and accidental suffocation'. The Coroner concluded that it was likely they were dead before Jindabyne police were even notified that they were missing.

The families of the four young men donated 12 EPIRBs (Emergency Position Indicating Radio Beacons) to Perisher Valley police as a positive and practical gesture. Their gift will ensure that others caught in the snow under the same circumstances will not perish.

8.
Billabong

Billabongs, creeks and mangroves are cool, calm places amidst the burning desert sands. They are also home to Australia's largest predator, the crocodile. These four stories show how overwhelmingly powerful the crocodile is. There's the story of the glamorous US model, trapped in waist-deep water between a cliff face and an approaching crocodile; the inspiring account of a 60-year-old woman who jumps onto the back of a 4.2 metre croc to save a friend; and there's the story of two young men who spend 22 hours clinging to a tree while the crocodile that took their mate waits patiently below. But first, the young German tourist who lost her life in a billabong, a story that shows how one brief moment is all it takes for a crocodile to strike.

CROCODILE

Crocodiles have been around for about 200 million years, so they are pretty much at home in their environment: the creeks, billabongs and coastal regions of northern Australia. They can walk on land—freshwater crocs can get to up to 17-18 kilometres per hour in a short burst of speed—but they are in their element in the water. In the water they are stealthy, strong and silent. They can float along with only their eyes and nostrils showing, making them extremely difficult to see. In deep water, they dive under, swim towards the surface in an arc and then suddenly strike, grabbing unwary birds, water buffalo and, occasionally, humans from below. They give their victims no time to cry out as they are dragged under and their lungs begin to fill with water. Most human deaths by crocodile are not from having limbs ripped off or being eaten alive. Most deaths by crocodile are from drowning.

THE TOUR GUIDE WHO MADE A FATAL MISTAKE

Name:	**Isabel von Jordan**
Age:	**23 years old**
Nationality:	**German**
Incident:	**Crocodile attack**
When:	**23 October 2002**
Where:	**Kakadu National Park, Northern Territory**
Outcome:	**Fatal**

This is the story of a highly experienced tour guide, two German sisters and a four-day wilderness adventure in Kakadu. It's the story of how the guide let his group go for a swim in a billabong on a warm balmy evening and how the night was shattered by a sudden vicious crocodile attack. It's the story of trying to piece together how this could possibly happen. Why did the guide give the go-ahead? Why did he let the travellers in his care swim in a waterhole that was home to at least eight large salt water crocodiles? Why did the group ignore the signs clearly warning of the danger?

A dream job

Glenn Robless was not a novice. He had thirteen years' experience in the tourism industry in the Northern Territory. According to a guide who worked with him, he was one of the best tour guides around. And he had a job that left desk-bound workers gasping. He got to take travellers through some of Australia's most awesome landscapes in Kakadu National Park, an area so ancient and extraordinary that it makes you rethink all your dreams. Here he would show visitors Aboriginal rock carvings tens of thousands of years old, beautiful bird life, breathtaking scenery. And every so often there would be bright yellow warning signs. WARNING. ACHTUNG. CROCODILES. Big bold letters in English, German and Japanese.

In October 2002, one such tour started up with eight or nine keen tourists, mainly young overseas backpackers. There was a young Brit from Essex, James Rothwell, who had been travelling around Australia for two-and-a-half months. There was a German woman, Carmen Willie. And there were two German sisters, Valerie and Isabel von Jordan. Valerie was 21 and Isabel was 23. To celebrate Isabel's graduation from an interior design course in Munich, they had set off on a three-month holiday through Thailand, Indonesia and on to Australia. It would be the holiday of a lifetime. But for all the wrong reasons.

Things had started to go wrong in Indonesia. October 2002 was when the island of Bali was rocked by a terrorist attack that left 202 dead including 88 Australians. Isabel and Valerie weren't in the Sari Club that night but they knew some who were. In the aftermath, Bali was chaotic and they didn't want to stay. So they decided to fly to Darwin, visit their injured friends now in Royal Darwin Hospital and then see the sights. They signed up for a four-day tour to Kakadu led by Glenn Robless.

It was Tuesday evening, the last night of their trip. The group were camping near Sandy Creek Billabong, about 35 kilometres south of Jabiru. There was a full moon over the water, the air was warm, the sky had a million stars. What could be more inviting than a midnight dip? There were at least three signs warning people not to swim because of crocodiles. But sometimes people ignore the signs …

Glenn knew there were crocodiles in the billabong. It was local knowledge that it was home to at least eight large saltwater crocs or 'salties'. He had taken groups there to wash, but he had never taken anyone swimming until that night. The thing that swayed him was a pile of mussel shells on the beach. His conclusion was that Aboriginal women had been in the water earlier to collect them, meaning the billabong must be safe. He shone his torch across the water, looking for 'eyeshine', the reflection of a croc's eyes in the beam of light.

Later, a traditional Aboriginal owner, Jessie Alderson, would tell the Coroner's court that 'eyeshine' is not a good test in a place like Sandy Billabong because it is so big.

The decision to swim

Glenn didn't see any sign of crocodiles. One rightly cautious backpacker asked him three times if it was safe to swim. Glenn replied that he was sure it was safe, but he had just wanted to check with a torch anyway. And with that, he jumped in.

Glenn seemed safety-conscious and sensible to the group; they trusted his judgement. A group of nine young people went for a swim. They splashed around, having a great time and dunking each other. One of the group, Andrew Waters from Britain, sat on the beach, trying to master the harder-than-it-looks art of playing the didgeridoo. After a while, Glenn got out of the water and went back to camp to invite another tour group to join in the fun.

Glenn was on his way back with some more campers when it happened out of the blue. A couple of swimmers felt something bump into them. But with all the energetic splashing, they didn't take much notice. James Rothwell thought one of his friends was playing a prank. Later he realised it was a crocodile that had bumped his leg.

'We were about 10 metres out from the shore, all within sight and arm's length of each other,' he recalled. 'I felt a bang on my leg and seconds later heard a girl scream and the girl went under the water. First of all I thought it was people mucking around …'

From the edge of the water, Andrew with his didgeridoo heard the screams. He too thought it was someone playing a bad joke. But then there was more yelling to get out of the water and a frenzied scramble to shore. The small group stood on the sand, dripping and scared. And when they counted everyone, they realised that one of them was missing.

'We got to the shore,' James said, 'shone torches on the water and we saw with the torches two red eyes going away from where the girl had just gone under and we saw the outline of a crocodile sort of swimming along the surface of the water.' The crocodile had struck without warning from below, clamping its jaws around Isabel von Jordan and dragging her under.

Hunt

One of the swimmers grabbed a satellite phone and rang for help. Police from Jabiru arrived on the scene. In no fit state to help, the tour group went back to their campsite and spent a dark night wondering why. Kakadu National Park rangers launched a massive hunt for the saltwater crocodile. They worked through the night—for seven long hours—searching the billabong for any trace of Isabel's body. They found the eight crocs known to inhabit the billabong but it was daybreak before they found what they were looking for.

6.15am. Rangers, torches in hand, were in a small boat in a tributary of the South Alligator River, about two kilometres from where Isabel had gone missing. It was still dark when their torchlight caught the form of a large saltwater crocodile. As the sun rose, everyone's worst fears were realised.

'We travelled towards it,' said Ranger Greg Ryan, 'and I noticed, as we came within metres of that crocodile … (that it) had what appeared to me to be a child.' It was the slightly built figure of Isabel von Jordan. The crocodile swam under the boat with the victim's body in its mouth.

It was a giant crocodile, 4.6 metres long and weighing about 500 kilograms. They harpooned it and it let go of the body. But an even larger croc then took up a defensive stance near the body, making it difficult to retrieve. The body was finally retrieved under about three metres of water by rangers using ropes and a hook, all the time being menaced by the second crocodile. Soon after, the German diplomatic representative in Darwin escorted Valerie von Jordan to Darwin airport where she caught a plane home to Munich.

Criminal charges?

Police considered charging Glenn Robless with manslaughter but this was later changed to the lesser charge of committing a dangerous act causing death. In 2003, he pleaded guilty to 'a dangerous omission causing death'. The Supreme Court found that the fault lay in 'the unforeseeable actions of an otherwise well-qualified tour guide, who made a horrible error of judgement'. He was given a three-year suspended jail sentence.

An inquest into the death of Isabel von Jordan in September 2004 found that the injuries she sustained from the crocodile bite—cutting her left lung and fracturing her ribs—were not life-threatening; it was found she had died from drowning.

THE GLAMOROUS MODEL AND THE CROCODILE

Name:	**Ginger Meadows**
Age:	**24 years old**
Nationality:	**American**
Incident:	**Crocodile attack**
When:	**29 March 1987**
Where:	**Prince Regent River, Western Australia**
Outcome:	**Fatal**

This story is an instant attention-grabber because it involves a beautiful young American model/actress. It doesn't matter that no-one seems to know exactly what acting or modelling she ever did, what matters is the image of a young starlet ending her life in the jaws of a crocodile. There are many references to Ginger Faye Meadows. She is consistently recorded in 'On This Day' chronologies for 29 March in Australian newspapers and is regularly referred to in books about crocodile attacks in Australia.

Those familiar with the story will know that Ginger Meadows jumped into a tidal pool and tried to outswim a crocodile. Which seems an incredible thing to do. But Ginger's actions that morning weren't as foolhardy as they first appear. In fact, on reading her story, you may come round to thinking that you might have done exactly the same thing.

Crocodile country

Ginger Meadows, from Snowmass Village, Colorado, was holidaying in Australia to get away from it all, especially a marriage that had gone sour. The ex-model was keen to see crocodile country in the north of Australia after having laughed her way through *Crocodile Dundee*, the blockbuster Oz movie of 1986.

She landed in Fremantle on the coast of Western Australia in late 1987, right in the middle of America's Cup fever. The fever pitch was pretty frenetic because Australia was defending the Cup for the first time ever, after *Australia II's* illustrious 1983 victory. Ginger enjoyed the atmosphere of the yacht-crazy port city and then continued on her way.

She took a ride on the Lady G, a 33-metre luxury cruiser heading north from Perth to Darwin. On board was the Captain, Bruce Fitzpatrick; the chef, Jane Burchett; engineer Steve Hilton and Madeleine Janes, the stewardess. It was a Sunday when they anchored near the mouth of Prince Regent River on the north coast of the Kimberley, about 250 kilometres NE of Derby. This river is known for two things: a magnificent freshwater waterfall and a large population of saltwater crocodiles.

They all went up-river in a smaller boat—known as a tender—to explore the region. They found the waterfall, the majestic Kings Cascade. Kings Cascade is a photographer's dream: a spectacular multi-tiered series of falls with water cascading down like icing on a massive wedding cake. Completing the picture was an idyllic tidal pool renewed by refreshing spring water all year round. The perfect place for a swim. Bruce Fitzpatrick brought the boat right up to the falls and the four aboard all climbed out onto the ledge and started to explore. Then Bruce took the boat up-river where he stayed and took some photos, looking back at the group against the cliff. He then came back, tied the boat up at the base of the waterfall and began to climb the 30 metre cliff face.

Ginger Meadows and Jane Burchett had just started to climb the cliff when Ginger realised she'd forgotten her camera, so they went back to the boat to get it. Bruce recalls seeing them in the boat when he was about halfway up the cliff. Having retrieved the camera, the two women swam back across the pool towards the rock ledge. Looking down from the cliff top, Bruce saw them in the water. He also saw a three-four metre crocodile swimming towards them.

Trapped

He shouted a warning and yelled out for Steve to get the boat and get the women out. Screaming, they scurried out of the water up onto the ledge under the waterfall. There they stood in waist-deep water. It was a nightmare scenario. A crocodile coming towards them and a sheer rock face behind. And they were not even on dry land, but in water where the crocodile is in its element. The two terrified women were trapped.

The crocodile was less than five metres away now. Jane tried to scare it off by throwing a shoe at it. The shoe hit the crocodile on the head which made it stop. Chillingly, it looked at them. And then it submerged.

Ginger panicked. Or miscalculated. Or both. She dived into the water, trying to reach the bank 25 metres away. She only made it a couple of metres. The crocodile lunged at her, grabbing her by the hips and dragging her down below the surface. It brought her up to the surface three times. The final time, she was lifeless.

Finding the body

Searching for the remains of a crocodile victim is complex and time-consuming. The search was called off late on Monday because of 10-metre tides and generator problems with the Lady G. It resumed at first light on Tuesday. Ginger's mutilated body was found that day on some tidal flats about one kilometre from where she was taken. Her remains were put in a body bag and transported back up the river in a smallish seven-metre boat. The boat had travelled about 15 kilometres up-river when a 3.5-metre crocodile leapt more than a metre out of the water, snapped at the body bag and ripped it open. The animal was frightened off by a gunshot.

Ginger's estranged husband, Duane McCaulley, from Aspen, Colorado spoke briefly with her parents before taking off for Australia. He arrived the day her body was found. He was unable to ID the body because of the state it was in. In cases like this, police rely on dental records and so Broome police contacted the US Consulate to arrange for her dental records to be made available. But her husband didn't think she had a single filling, such is the curse of perfect teeth.

Duane McCaulley accompanied the body to Perth for the post-mortem. Apparently, he was so distressed that the flight attendant and her boyfriend let him stay at their place for a few days afterwards to recover. Then he flew home to the US with the remains of his estranged wife.

In the weeks that followed, cruise organisations received a number of enquiries from overseas tourists who wanted to go to the Kimberley—even though they had no idea where it was—to see the spot where the crocodile attack had taken place. Today, tourist information for the region sometimes refers to the 'infamous' Kings Cascade, mentioning the scene of the attack as some kind of strange tourist attraction. Some of the information makes no reference to the incident at all.

Ginger Meadows would have celebrated her twenty-fifth birthday on 30 March, the day after she died.

THE GRANDMA WHO JUMPED ON A CROCODILE

Name:	**Alicia Sorohan**
Age:	**60 years old**
Nationality:	**Australian**
Incident:	**Crocodile attack**
When:	**11 October 2004**
Where:	**Cape York Peninsula, Queensland**
Outcome:	**Non-fatal**

What is bravery? Sometimes it's planning something courageous and carrying out your plan. Other times it's jumping in and doing something without really thinking at all. And that's what this story is about. Instinctive reaction. Leaping before you look. Putting the lives of others before your own because it seems like a good idea at the time. This is the story of a very brave lady who jumps on the back of a giant crocodile to save a family friend, nearly gets her arm ripped off and then has to endure the agony of a seemingly never-ending five hour drive to get medical help. And even then, this amazing woman continues to claim that anyone would have done the same under the circumstances ...

Camping holiday

Bill and Alicia Sorohan loved getting away from it all and heading off to some of Queensland's most beautiful and remote places. They'd been having camping adventure holidays for more than 20 years and for the last five years had chosen Bathurst Bay, a popular fishing spot 250 kilometres north of Cooktown on the Cape York Peninsula.

This year was no different. A contingent of five four-wheel drives took off loaded up with supplies, tents, petrol, two dinghies and trail bikes. There was Bill and Alicia, their son Jason, their daughter Melinda and her husband, Wayne, along with their friends Andrew and Diane Kerr. There were also some little children in tow: Bill and Alicia's two granddaughters Kaitlyn, 6, and Rhiannan, 3; and Andrew and Diane's little baby boy, Kelly. The group was looking forward to a relaxing three-week break, fishing, bushwalking and trail biking by the waters of Bathurst Bay.

It was the middle of the night. All was quiet. About 20 metres from the water's edge, five tents housed seven adults and three children blissfully dead to the world. But in the hours of pre-dawn, not every creature was asleep. At about 4am, a massive 4.2-metre crocodile emerged from the water and made a beeline for one particular tent.

Strangely, it ignored the tent with all the food. Instead, it lumbered up the bank and went straight for one of the furthest tents from the water. Inside the tent was Andrew Kerr, his wife Diane and their 3-month-old baby boy, Kelly.

Diane woke up suddenly. She heard a heavy thud outside the tent. Through the netting, she was shocked to find a crocodile staring at her with gleaming yellow eyes. 'There's a croc, Andrew!' was all she managed to say. At that, the crocodile burst through the tent flaps, ripping them effortlessly. It lunged at Andrew, sank its teeth into his leg and began to drag him out of the tent.

Andrew screamed. 'Get the baby!' he yelled as the crocodile pulled him outside. Diane grabbed Kelly with one hand. With the other, she desperately tried to keep hold of her husband. And she screamed her heart out.

Bill and Alicia were in the nearest tent. They grabbed a torch and ran towards the commotion. Alicia's first thought was that something was wrong with the baby; Bill thought it must be a dingo. They ran around the tent in different directions and Alicia got there first. The baby was OK, Diane gushed, but the crocodile had Andrew.

Alicia saves the day

Without hesitation, Alicia jumped onto the back of the 300 kilogram crocodile. It instantly released Andrew, threw its head back and smashed into Alicia's nose with its jaws. With the impact, she lost balance and toppled off its back onto the sand. Her son-in-law, Wayne, saw the whole thing. 'I couldn't believe it,' he later said, 'Jason's mother was on top of this crocodile. It flung her off and then grabbed her arm.'

The crocodile struck again, sinking its teeth into Alicia's right arm and thrashing about wildly. Alicia was screaming, 'It's got my arm!' Struggling on the ground, face to face with the enormous creature, Alicia thought her days were numbered. 'I was lying in the sand looking at him eye to eye, and I thought this was it.'

Jason Sorohan came to the rescue with a high-calibre pistol. His only thought was to save his mother. Bill was there too, with an axe, ready to smash the croc's skull if the gun misfired. Jason jumped on the croc, dug his knees into its scaly back and fired two shots into the back of its head.

Alicia heard the gun go off but she didn't register what it was. All she knew was that the croc's grip on her arm suddenly loosened and she felt the life go out of her much stronger opponent. She couldn't recall later how she got her arm out of the croc's mouth, but she knew it wasn't a pretty sight. At least the menace was gone. The croc was dead.

Injuries

Alicia's injuries were grotesque. 'Her arm was just shocking. You could put your fist in it, that was the size of the hole,' said Bill. Her arm was hanging by a few centimetres of skin and there were fears that she would lose it. Andrew too was in terrible shape with a badly broken leg, a broken arm and cuts all over his body. They needed to get medical help but Andrew couldn't be moved; his injuries were too severe.

They bandaged Alicia's arm. The only thing to do was hop into one of the four-wheel drives and drive to the nearest ranger's station at Lakefield, five hours away. It was a rough and very uncomfortable journey of 120 kilometres. But despite the difficulties, Alicia was awake the whole time, talking, worrying about everyone but herself. And she did not complain once.

Meanwhile back at the campsite, the family found someone further up the beach with an emergency beacon and radio. The Royal Flying Doctor Service picked up the distress call and arranged to pick up both Andrew and Alicia who were flown to Cairns Base Hospital.

They both recovered, slowly. Alicia spent ten days in hospital as well as many more months in and out of physiotherapy. Fears that she might lose her arm were unfounded; when she came out of surgery, she quipped that she was surprised to see she still had it. She now has two permanent plates and twelve screws in her arm and is unable to turn her hand properly but it could have been a lot worse. And son-in-law Wayne summed it up nicely when he said, 'She deserves an award of some kind.'

Alicia did receive acknowledgement of her selfless act. On 26 August 2005, she was awarded the Star of Courage, which recognises Australian citizens for acts of outstanding bravery. And who should present the award but the Crocodile Hunter himself, Steve Irwin.

TWO MATES STUCK UP A TREE

Name:	**Brett Mann**
Age:	**22 years old**
Nationality:	**Australian**
Incident:	**Crocodile attack**
When:	**21 December 2003**
Where:	**Finniss River, Northern Territory**
Outcome:	**Fatal**

The bonds of mateship are strong. Young blokes forge friendships by doing things together and sharing adventures. The three friends in this story are just like that. Born and bred Territorians with a great love for the freedom, beauty and wildness of the land. This is their story. It's a story of being in the wrong place at the wrong time. And it's the story of how in an instant your whole world can come crashing down. A family is left bereft, friends must come to grips with losing their best mate and a young man is gone forever. Who could have known that on that very ordinary Sunday, three mates would go out but only two would come back?

Three mates

Quad bikes grab the imagination of the young and adventurous. Known as ATVs, or All Terrain Vehicles, the name says it all. They go over all kinds of surfaces with a roar: water, dirt trails, muddy river banks. They're like a cross between a motorbike and a small car. Or a motocross bike with four wheels. Even for the complete beginner, the controls are pretty easy to master. And they are a real adrenalin-pumping way to spend an afternoon. That's just what three mates were doing the Sunday before Christmas, 2003. Quad biking along the Finniss River, 80 kilometres SW of Darwin in the Northern Territory. Shaun Blowers and Ashley McGough were both 19 years old. Brett Mann was a 22-year-old diesel mechanic from Howard Springs. He'd been the Northern Territory's third-year 'Apprentice of the Year' the year before. The three were great mates. In fact, Shaun's father Greg jokingly called Brett his adopted son because he was round at their place so often.

That Sunday afternoon everything got covered in mud. Brett, Shaun and Ashley went down to the riverbank to wash themselves. They were mucking around the way they usually did, spraying each other and splashing the water over their clothes, boots and faces. Suddenly, part of the bank gave way. Brett lost his footing, tumbled into the water and was swept away by the strong current.

Quick as a flash, Shaun and Ashley jumped in. They swam along, pushed by the fast-flowing water, unaware of another presence in the river. A silent saltwater crocodile.

They managed to get to Brett and grabbed hold of him. They were helping him back to the safety of the bank when the crocodile came into view. It had been hiding behind the rushes. Shaun waded past without seeing it. But Ashley saw it. And as he watched, the crocodile suddenly lunged at Brett, seized him by the shoulder and dragged him under.

Ashley screamed, 'Croc, croc!' and he and Shaun swam wildly to the closest thing that could get them out of the water. It was a tree, standing in the middle of the river, about 50 metres from the bank. They shimmied up it and then, clinging to the branches, shaking and in shock, they looked down. Frantically, they searched the surface of the water, looking for Brett, for some sign that he was still there. The top of his head, his hand, some bubbles, anything. But there was nothing. Not even the sound of splashing or a cry piercing the stillness.

The crocodile was nowhere in sight. And Brett had vanished. But less than two minutes later, the croc resurfaced holding Brett's body in its jaws. It swam up to the tree. It almost seemed to be showing off its prized catch. And then it swam away. But moments later something stirred. The crocodile turned around and began to swim back.

Late that afternoon, the young men's families and friends began to wonder where the three had got to. Some of their mates reckoned they might have been stranded by floodwaters. After all, it was the wet season and the river was pretty swollen. When they hadn't returned by 7pm, a group went out searching. They knew where the three boys usually went quad bike riding, so they were pretty sure they'd find them. They searched all night, almost until dawn, but found nothing.

At 4am they all went home, failure weighing heavily on their minds and bodies. It was too early to raise the alarm, so they had a couple of hours of sleep and then told the boys' parents they'd had no luck. Doubts began to surface. Perhaps they weren't trapped by rising waters, perhaps something worse had happened. The boys' parents rang the police.

Two in a tree

Afterwards no-one was able to explain why the crocodile came back. Having taken Brett Mann, it surely had no need for further prey. But the two mates had the distinct feeling that they were being stalked, and who could blame them? So Shaun and Ashley did the only thing they could. They stayed put all night, high up in the branches, about 50 metres from shore in the middle of the river. And underneath them, the crocodile lurked all night long.

Away from the street lights, there was nothing comforting about the bush. Just coldness and fear and darkness so thick that even though they were within an arm's reach of one another, they couldn't see each other. They knew all they had to do was keep awake. If they fell asleep, they would fall into the water, perhaps into the jaws of the very patient crocodile below. Shaun held onto Ashley's foot through the night; and they kept a constant check on each other to make sure neither of them nodded off.

Monday morning dawned. The crocodile played a cruel game of cat and mouse. It would glide out of view and the two boys would consider coming down. But then it would loom into view again. Taunting them. Daring them. They stayed put. Clinging to that tree, holding on for their very lives in strong winds and driving rain.

Emergency teams, including the Northern Territory Tactical Response Group, spent the day looking for the young men in a rescue helicopter. Finally at 3pm they were spotted in the tree. Two personnel and a life raft were winched down into the river, slightly upstream from the trapped pair. The rescue workers paddled downstream towards the tree, using branches and swim fins for oars. That was the easy bit. Then they had to talk the two young men into coming down. Not surprisingly, they weren't all that keen. In fact, one of the rescuers remembers the first thing they said was, 'You guys are bloody mad!'.

Eventually, the pair were coaxed down from the tree and the four of them successfully made their way in the life raft to the riverbank. Shaun and Ashley were safe and on dry land after having spent an incredible 22 hours clinging to a tree. From there, the two young men were winched into the helicopter and flown to Royal Darwin Hospital, where they were treated for shock and hypothermia.

Shaun's father Greg, who joined the search, was overwhelmed with gratitude when his son was found safe: 'I think I'm going to appreciate him a hell of a lot more than I used to,' he said.

Killing the croc

Meanwhile, National Parks and Wildlife rangers and police with high-powered semi-automatics went out searching for Brett Mann's body, with orders to shoot the croc if they found it. Bad weather and fading light forced them to abandon the hunt but they resumed the next day.

About a week later, the search for the elusive croc continued. A 3.8-metre crocodile was shot by a ranger just 20 metres from where Brett had been attacked. The body sank in the muddy water, but officials were hopeful that when it resurfaced it would prove to be the crocodile. Chances were good: crocs were territorial and two large creatures in the same vicinity was unlikely.

While it may seem futile or even tasteless to keep on hunting for a crocodile, it did make sense. The aim of the search was to try and locate Brett's body so that his family could have some kind of closure. But his body was not found and may never be found. The search was officially closed nearly a year later when searchers returned to the area but found no trace of Brett Mann or the crocodile.

One week after the search ended was the painful first anniversary of Brett's death. His mother, Chris, said that the only positive thing to come out of the loss was how his mates, Shaun and Ashley, had come to terms with the tragedy. Before he died, Brett had spent much of his spare time working on a mud racer. His mates saw to it that they got it up and running.

'The mud racer was Brett's dream,' she said, 'and they've built on it, which means a lot to us. They are very special to me and I'm very proud of them for keeping Brett's memory alive.'

Lee Kernaghan and the muster

It's now spring. A time of renewal and hope. Ashley's mum, Kay, writes to Brett's hero, country singer Lee Kernaghan, wondering if he would dedicate a song to Brett at the Darwin City Muster in September.

Lee Kernaghan doesn't just devote a song to Brett. He dedicates his whole performance to Brett, celebrating his life and acknowledging the bonds of those who have grown up in the bush. How important it is to stand together, be proud of where you come from and remember that we are all part of the same humanity.

It is a fitting gesture to one of Lee Kernaghan's greatest fans. You see, Brett shook Lee's hand at a muster the year before and didn't wash it for a whole week. And that's how it is: the dirt, the mud, the bonds forever forged, the quad bikes and the Territory.

9.
Outback

The Australian Outback is sublime, breathtaking and indifferent to human suffering. Here you'll read stories of people who experience their own kind of hell in the desert, some surviving, some not. There's the story of a woman who dies alone in the desert on the day she is due to fly home; the tale of a Japanese motorcyclist who runs out of petrol in the middle of nowhere; and the extraordinary account of two British men stranded at the same time in different parts of the Outback.

Then there's the fascinating saga of Robert Bogucki who sets off on a spiritual quest across the Great Sandy Desert, not realising that he has unwittingly set off a massive search operation. You can read and ponder over the justifiably notorious story of Azaria Chamberlain, the baby taken by a dingo at Uluru in 1980, which links to a story that you may not know: the death of a man at Uluru in 1986. But first, the tragedy of Gabriele Grossmueller, who tried to walk for help in the blazing desert sun in South Australia.

HEAT EXHAUSTION (HYPERTHERMIA) AND EXPOSURE

EXTINGUISHING THE HUMAN SPIRIT

Name:	**Gabriele Grossmueller**
Age:	**28 years old**
Nationality:	**Austrian**
Incident:	**Heat exhaustion (hyperthermia) and exposure**
When:	**12 December 1998**
Where:	**Lake Eyre, South Australia**
Outcome:	**Fatal**

What would prompt you to set off on foot across one of the most inhospitable landscapes in the world? When temperatures are in the mid to high 40s, when there is no shade, no trees and patches of earth are scorched to black? Why on earth would anyone attempt to walk for help? Panic is the only imaginable reason. In a strange place under great stress, it would be easy to feel completely out of your comfort zone. The glaring heat would sap your energy and muddle your thinking. Even if you tried to suppress it, panic would raise its ugly head, eating away at reason until all your thoughts were terrifying.

This is the story of a young woman who died alone in the burning desert sands of South Australia. In her failed quest for help, she walked past water bores, water troughs and a 400-litre water tank that was at least half full. Her boyfriend, who sat it out in their hired four-wheel drive, lived. If only she had stayed with the car …

Karl and Gabriele's holiday

In October 1998, two young, well-educated Austrians flew into Darwin, capital of the Northern Territory. Karl Goeschka was a research assistant at Vienna University of Technology; Gabriele Grossmueller was a medical student. They'd been together for 11 years. They picked up a campervan and went on a whirlwind tour of Oz: the Northern Territory, Queensland, New South Wales, Victoria and Tasmania.

Sunday 6 December. Back on the mainland, they camped out at Coward Springs, a scenic spot in South Australia with soothing hot water springs from the Great Artesian Basin and vast wetlands attracting a wonderful array of bird life.

Monday 7 December. They drove north to William Creek, permanent population of about 15, a pinprick somewhere in the middle of the Oodnadatta Track. This settlement is in the middle of South Australia's Anna Creek Station, the biggest pastoral lease in the world. There's a sign with skull and crossbones that says, 'Anna Creek Station track to various places including LAKE EYRE NTH 73. Low traffic track. Low vehicles should check in at William Creek Hotel BEFORE traversing!'

So they did. Karl talked to the pub owner's son and told him that they would be heading off to explore Lake Eyre along the Halligan Bay track. Their plan was to camp there overnight and be back by noon the next day. The son looked around for the hotel's 'Search and Rescue' (SAR) book but couldn't find it. So he started a new log and wrote the couple's details down including their ETA (Estimated Time of Arrival) back at the hotel. He told them that if something happened someone would come out looking for them. And if they didn't return by the time they said, he'd 'hit the panic button'. (*Inquest into the Death of Gabriele Grossmueller*, Section 3.5, 2000). They left, safe in the knowledge that they were logged in the book. But their sense of security was misplaced.

Karl and Gabriele set off in their four-wheel drive along the 70 or so kilometres of bumpy roads to the camping site. They had good supplies of food and water, and quite a few booklets that gave advice on survival in an emergency. All the booklets said the same thing:

- Do not leave the vehicle
- Stay in the shade
- Conserve energy

If only they had both taken that advice.

Along the way to Halligan Bay, you drive past ABC Bay where the ground is covered in strange small black stones, giving the impression that the whole earth is scorched. Some might call it an ugly barren landscape, but as you leave the desolate blackness behind, the sands turn to pink and it is altogether a softer land.

Karl and Gabriele arrived at Halligan Bay at about 5.30pm but as they reversed their vehicle, they got bogged in the sand. They had no real training in how to handle four-wheel drives in soft sands. Karl knew that deflating the tyres would help, but he didn't deflate them sufficiently. The vehicle was also in axle-twist: the front and rear axles were at an angle to each other and the differentials weren't locked, so there was no traction.

Bogged

Tuesday 8 December. The couple tried to dig themselves out using cups as shovels; they tried a suitcase placed under the wheel to get traction. Nothing worked. Tellingly, the Senior Constable who found the vehicle one week later didn't have any problems at all. He deflated the tyres, spent ten minutes digging out the sand, then drove out effortlessly.

Wednesday 9 December. Hot, stuck and alone. The full impact of how isolated they were was sinking in. Temperatures in the region over the next few days averaged 40.93°C in the shade. Out in the open it was 15-20° hotter. In Karl Goeshcka's words, they became 'really frightened' (ibid, Section 3.8). The words of the pub owner's son ringing in their ears didn't help. They remembered him telling them that in such a place, they may not see anyone for six weeks. It was too early to panic, but they wanted to do something. So at 4pm they decided to walk back to William Creek along a corrugated track with no shade. Anyone who knows anything about Outback survival would know this was inadvisable in the extreme.

They walked until late that night, then they put up a tent and rested until pre-dawn.

Thursday 10 December, 2am. More walking, knowing that first light would bring ferocious temperatures. Karl began to feel ill and couldn't keep going. Gabriele reasoned that she was better at tolerating the heat, she was a better walker on flat ground and she would use less water. She wanted to continue; Karl did not. He stayed with the tent and three litres of water. At 4am, Gabriele set out by herself, taking the remaining nine litres.

For the rest of that day, Karl stayed in the tent in extreme temperatures. Fearing he would die and with only one litre of water left, that night he began the walk back to the car.

Friday 11 December, 2am. Karl made it back to the car where there was plenty of food and water. There he waited. And waited. But no-one came.

Forgotten souls

Saturday 12 December. Back at the William Creek Hotel, the pub owner's son had been busy the past few days with a group of tourists who'd broken down and been stranded for four days. Usually his dad checked the SAR book every night to see if anyone was missing but his dad was away. The pub owner's son left for Melbourne without checking the book or mentioning it to any other member of staff. If Karl was relying on the SAR book being read and responded to—a reasonable assumption—he was let down badly. No-one would be out looking for them. No one realised they were in trouble. Gabriele Grossmueller and Karl Goeschka were forgotten souls.

Sitting in the four-wheel drive, contemplating the last few days, Karl began to write. Pages and pages indicating that he thought he was going to die.

Tuesday 15 December. Two German tourists, Christoph Kupper and Hans-Martin Kieser, were driving along a track off the Oodnadatta Track about 11 kilometres south of William Creek, heading towards Lake Eyre.

About 30 kilometres along, they saw a body lying on the side of the road, so badly decomposed that it was impossible to identify. Beside it was a rucksack with 1.5 litres of water in a two litre bottle, another five litres of water and a bottle with 80mls of urine. There was a note in German and English in part saying 'HELP!' and describing her terrible plight as 'still trying to get out of this hell …' (ibid, Section 1.5).

The Germans raced back to William Creek Hotel and notified the owner, who called police and arranged to meet Senior Constable Paul Liersch from Marree. They drove together to the body, which was taken back to William Creek by two detectives from Coober Pedy Criminal Investigation Branch. Senior Constable Liersch and the hotel owner then drove further on to a junction in the road where they found a note scrawled by Gabriele taped to a sign. They took the SE road and found nothing, so they returned and drove NE. There they found the remains of another note she had left. As they got closer to the shores of Lake Eyre, they found shoe prints and tyre marks which they followed to Halligan Bay. Parked near a tourist shelter was a land cruiser, and inside was a very distressed Karl Goeschka.

What goes through someone's mind under these circumstances? The pub owner's son will have to live with the knowledge that he wrote down the couple's travel plans but never gave them a second thought. Karl Goeschka will be haunted for the rest of his life by he and Gabriele's fateful decision to part ways. If he had stopped her, if he had convinced her to stay, if they had both returned to the car …

And Gabriele Grossmueller? Dying of heat exhaustion, alone in a desolate land, she would have felt a terrifying solitude that few have known. She may well have thought it was crazy to keep walking—it's insane, but I must. What is it about the human spirit? We want to act. We want to make things right. We want to live.

A simple white cross stands on Halligan Bay track near Armistice Bore marking the place where Gabriele Grossmueller perished.

THE WOMAN WHO VISITED MUTITJULU

Name:	**Ethel Hetherington**
Age:	**52 years old**
Nationality:	**British**
Incident:	**Heat Exhaustion (hyperthermia)**
When:	**27 October 2004**
Where:	**Yulara, Northern Territory**
Outcome:	**Fatal**

Tragic deaths are not just the realm of outdoor adventurers and chronic risk-takers. They can come to ordinary people. Like Ethel Hetherington. Ethel lived in a close-knit community in Great Broughton, Cumbria in the UK. Her husband Jimmy—in his 70s—had multiple sclerosis, and her sister-in-law had recently been diagnosed with the same condition. She had two grown-up children, 31 and 16 years old. She was a charity worker for the local community and by all accounts was active, cheerful and fun to be around. She had a treat in store which might have been Shirley Valentine's second choice if the Greek Isles didn't work out: a three-week dream holiday in Australia. Better still, she took off to see the sights with her cousin and her cousin's husband, leaving hubby and kids at home. And she had the time of her life until the very last night of her holiday.

Last night in Australia

It's a Monday night at Yulara, the unique resort town near Uluru. It could be any night; days of the week don't make much of a difference out here. The land, the colours and the tour guide schedules have a certain timelessness about them.

In the bar of the Outback Pioneer Hotel, three happy Brits were enjoying their last night in Australia. Ethel Hetherington, along with her cousin and cousin's husband, were at the end of their three-week holiday. When the others went to bed at 9.30pm, Ethel stayed put. She got chatting with some young men from Mutitjulu, the no-alcohol Aboriginal community of 350 people about 19 kilometres SE of Uluru. But as to what Ethel did next and why, no-one will ever really know.

Only hotel guests are permitted to drink at Yulara. Perhaps her new friends were asked to leave. It's not clear, but what is clear is that her stay in Australia had sparked an interest in Aboriginal culture. So perhaps she saw a chance to see Mutitjulu, an authentic Aboriginal community. And after all, it was her last night at Yulara. Mutitjulu is on Aboriginal land, which requires a permit to enter. But the locals were happy to give her a lift so she took off on a late-night visit.

It's virtually impossible to deduce how long she stayed or what she did; but she seems to have stayed there for a few hours. As for what she saw or felt, it is likely that she was in for a shock. Nothing comforting or familiar. A deep isolation that comes from being white, English, female and a long way from home. Apparently Ethel left the community without telling anyone and started to walk back to her hotel.

The next day, Ethel's cousin raised the alarm when she had not returned to her hotel room. Aboriginal trackers, police, resort staff and volunteers searched the area but failed to find any sign of her. An air search also proved fruitless. At first light on Wednesday, more police were flown in.

And now the story zooms in on one particular area to the east of Mutitjulu. There is a remote dirt road, known as Old Petermann Road, that leads to Curtin Springs, the nearest town to Yulara. Just after 10am, some Mutitjulu people returning home from Curtin Springs made a sobering discovery: a woman's body lying on the track.

Her final movements

Ethel Hetherington's body was found 36 hours after she had last been seen at Yulara. Police were unable to give the cause of death, only that she seemed to have done an 'enormous amount of walking'. Acting Commander Don Fry said, 'There's no obvious signs of foul play …

but there's a lot of work to do within the community to trace her last movements from Yulara to where she was found.'

The puzzle was how Ethel Hetherington managed to get to the spot where she was found. Her body was found 22 kilometres away from Mutitjulu on a track heading east to Curtin Springs. But her hotel at Yulara was to the west. Why had she been walking in the opposite direction? Police converged on the Yulara resort to piece together her final movements.

One possible scenario is that when Ethel woke up early on Tuesday morning she realised she had a lunchtime flight to catch. So she decided to make her own way back to the hotel. She was in a remote region. She covered a lot of ground but headed in the wrong direction. It's likely that early morning exposure, ferocious daytime heat and lack of water took their toll.

Various tests—including toxicology tests—were carried out to determine the probable cause of death. In the early stages of investigation, the police were working on the assumption that her death was a tragic accident. In the end, the autopsy failed to establish a cause of death. The investigation was handed over to the Coroner.

Coroner's report

Ultimately, there was nothing sinister about Ethel Hetherington's death. In July 2005, the NT Coroner sent the results of the investigation to her family in England but declined to publish the findings in Australia, deeming an inquest into the cause of her death unnecessary. Interestingly, the Coroner's findings were later released, allegedly to 'quell speculation'. It was found that Ethel Hetherington had died of hyperthermia, or over-heating, 22 kilometres east of Mutitjulu near Uluru in October 2004. There were no suspicious circumstances surrounding her death.

Hundreds of mourners farewelled Ethel Hetherington at Christ Church, Broughton. Regulars at the Sun Dial pub in Little Broughton paid tribute to her with a minute's silence; and a minute's silence for her was observed at the start of Broughton's annual charity event, the Magnificent Seven Cycle Ride. In her lifetime, Ethel had tirelessly worked for various charities, and had raised hundred of pounds by turning her fortieth and fiftieth birthdays into charity events. So her friends and family decided to carry on the tradition and turn what would have been Ethel's fifty-third birthday into something special. The resulting concert had two wonderful outcomes: it raised £615 for breast cancer research and was a joyful celebration of Ethel's life.

DEHYDRATION

DIARY OF A MAD MAX

Name:	**Masa Hira Ono**
Age:	**22 years old**
Nationality:	**Japanese**
Incident:	**Dehydration**
When:	**Found 2 January 1994**
Where:	**Laverton, Western Australia**
Outcome:	**Non-fatal**

This story is set in the mid 1990s when Japanese youth were going crazy about Max Rockatansky, aka Mad Max. When the *Mad Max* movies were released in Japan, a new cult hero was born. Max, Jim the Goose and all the gang with their wild futuristic clothes and throbbing metal machines captured a certain something you just couldn't find in downtown Tokyo. In this story, you'll read about a self-styled Japanese 'road warrior' of sorts who sets off on his own personal crusade to ride a motorbike across a remote part of Western Australia. But instead of raising hell as he roars across the barren Mad Max-esque landscape, he gets hopelessly stuck, his gears go wonky and he runs out of petrol. There he is in a real life and death scenario but his survival skills—or lack of—show the world that he honestly doesn't have a clue. What would Max do? Certainly not what this young Japanese student did.

The Mad Max obsession

Imagine it's 1993, you are a young Japanese tourist on holiday in Australia. You could visit the Sydney Opera House (yawn), fly to the Gold Coast (bigger yawn) or go on a five-day Mad Max extravaganza, specially designed for Japanese Max devotees. You would visit the National Motor

Museum in Adelaide and see *the* car; ride north on your specially-hired Kawasaki to Coober Pedy and Moon Plain to see the real live film locations and then head off to Gladstone, South Australia. Here you would settle back—together with Steve 'Jim the Goose' Bisley and 100 friendly Adelaide bikies—to watch the Max movies up on the big screen in an abandoned drive-in specially reopened for the event. You would get to dress up in studded leather and re-enact your favourite scenes from the movie. All for only $3000, even less if you have a fetching enough mohawk—you got a discount if you had Mad Max-inspired hair.

You had to be a fairly avid fan to splash out on such a tour. But many Japanese—young and old—came to Australia in the 1990s to experience its vastness, subconsciously or consciously drawn by the allure of Max Rockatansky. Many of these visitors didn't realise exactly how big Australia was, such as the young man who wanted to hire a bike and ride from Sydney to Perth and back. In three days.

Masa Hira Ono didn't aspire to anything quite that impossible. In fact, he set himself an entirely achievable goal. The only trouble was, this unassuming young man went about it in entirely the wrong way. Hence the unflattering headlines when the story unfolded: 'Desert tourist stupid: police'.

It all started when Masa bought a Honda 250cc in Sydney. He wanted to ride way out, see the desert country, ride back and jump on a plane bound for Japan. That's how one Wednesday in late 1993, this 22-year-old English language student found himself in the Gibson Desert, nearly 156, 000 square kilometres of red sand and mulga bounded on the north by the Great Sandy Desert and on the south by the Great Victoria Desert. Having ridden as far west as he wanted, he now wanted to head back east. With Carnegie Station as his starting point, Masa set off east along the Gunbarrell Highway, an arduous and unsealed stretch of road. His destination was Warburton, just over 450 kilometres away. He took four litres of water with him which, in anyone's language, is not enough.

Early on Thursday, his bike rack fell off. So he dumped all his supplies by the side of the road and headed back to Carnegie. It's not too hard to guess what happened next. He ran out of petrol. And, of course, his spare fuel was back by the side of the road where he'd abandoned it, 70 kilometres away. Masa was in the middle of nowhere with nothing. Actually, that isn't quite true. In one of those wild flukes of nature, he had broken down just 10 metres from a water bore. There he was, out in the middle of a desert, steps away from a life-saving water supply. There was even a drinking cup attached with a cord. The bore had a sticker marked 'Water is available at 46m' but Masa couldn't understand the sign. Another sticker had the name of a radio station. So Masa wrongly concluded that the bore was not a bore at all, but an FM Radio transmitter.

Stay out of the sun!

Friday. New Year's Eve and most of the country was getting ready to watch fireworks and party or preferably both. All Masa knew was that it was stinking hot. Temperatures were around 41°C in the shade and 50°C in the sun, dropping to an uncomfortable 23°C during the night. Masa didn't realise that finding shade was not a luxury but a necessity. He didn't seem to understand that shade would not just help him feel more comfortable, it could well save his life. He sat out in the direct sun, unable to think, unable to move, slowly going delirious.

No food. There was plenty of water nearby but Masa did not recognise it. Aside from the bore water which he had neglected, there was also a muddy pool staring him in the face. But by now he was too far gone to know that he needed it desperately. He saw only muddy water and thought he would get sick if he drank it. He didn't know at that point that he was slipping perilously into a state of delirium. He didn't know that you can boil water to kill germs. But hell, if you're dying of thirst in the middle of the desert, who cares about germs?

Saturday, New Year's Day. Masa was in a bad way. Dehydration, sunstroke and delirium are not the best way to start the new year. Water was within reach but he didn't drink, couldn't drink, didn't know he had to. By this time he could hardly move, he was so overcome by exhaustion. And he certainly wasn't coherent enough to realise that he should try and find shade. At some point on New Year's Day he thought something that the Easybeats had sung decades before: 'I think I'm gonna lay me down and die …' . He decided to kill himself, but he couldn't figure out a way to do it. Which is just as well because, that evening, a station worker at Warburton had called police to report him missing. Help was on the way.

Waiting to die

Sunday. By 8am it was already 35°C. Police knew Masa's approximate whereabouts and they were hot on his trail. They arrived to find an astonishing sight. There he was, in T-shirt, shorts and socks, totally delirious, lying on his back in the blazing sun on the edge of a muddy pool, dangling his tootsies in the water. By all accounts, he was simply waiting to die, but why was he still wearing his socks? In the words of Constable Phil Brenton, the young man was completely 'buggered' (*The Daily Telegraph Mirror*, p. 8, 4 January 1994).

His amazed rescuers moved him into the shade and gave him re-hydration tablets. They couldn't believe he was alive. After all, he seemed to have done everything in his power to not survive. Poor Masa was so weak that he needed to be propped up; he told police he hadn't been able to move for two days. He would have been dead by nightfall.

The poor weak road warrior was carried back to the police vehicle and driven 60 kilometres south to the Tjirrkarli community. From there, a nurse came to take him to Warburton. He recovered after a couple of days and was well enough to zoom out of town back to Sydney. And then catch a plane out, back to the sanity of Japan.

What Mad Max would have thought of him, we'll never know. But we do have the wise words of Constable Brenton: 'He could have survived for quite a while if he had used his head or had some sort of survival skills. It was just plain stupidity which nearly killed him.' (*The Sydney Morning Herald*, p. 3, 4 September 1994)

LIFE AND DEATH DECISIONS IN WESTERN AUSTRALIA

Name:	**Thomas Henry Sykes**
Age:	**35 years old**
Nationality:	**British**
Incident:	**Dehydration**
When:	**Found 11 December 2003**
Where:	**Great Sandy Desert, Western Australia**
Outcome:	**Fatal**

Name:	**Howard Holdsworth**
Age:	**54 years old**
Nationality:	**British**
Incident:	**Lost**
When:	**Found 10 December 2003**
Where:	**Broome, Western Australia**
Outcome:	**Non-fatal**

This is the story of two men who never even knew each other but were linked by circumstance. They were both British, both on holidays in Australia at the same time and both travelling alone. They both chose to explore the remote north-west of Western Australia solo and both got into trouble in harsh, life-threatening environments. Sadly, following these remarkable similarities, their stories diverge. One man survives and one man dies. And the reasons why are very clear.

Ambitious plans

Thomas Sykes, a property developer from London, was someone who'd been known to do a crazy thing or two. So when he came to Australia he wanted to do something big. He spent six weeks travelling round, hired a four-wheel drive in Queensland and made his way across to Western Australia, but that wasn't enough. Now he wanted to do the ultimate:

cross the country from west to east. Starting off from Port Hedland, he would head to Alice Springs in the Red Centre—a distance of over 3000 kilometres—and then travel the rest of the way to the east coast. Destination: Sydney. A mind-boggling journey of around 6000 kilometres through some of the most unforgiving terrain imaginable. He was warned more than once before he set out that the trip was risky.

Monday 8 December. Thomas set off to drive the 600 kilometres from Broome to Port Hedland, the first leg of his journey. He'd been offered an Outback safety kit when he hired his vehicle but he didn't take it. At least he did have plenty of water.

Tuesday 9 December. The second leg of his journey. Another 600 kilometre stretch of not terribly good dirt road to Punmu, a remote Aboriginal community on the eastern shores of Lake Dora. Remote is no exaggeration. Postal deliveries are by air and Port Hedland is the nearest town. When the road's passable. The climate out this way is not everyone's cup of tea: temperatures hover around 30°C in winter and hit 50°C in the summertime. Dust storms and willie-willies (sort of mini cyclones) are common throughout the year. But to be fair, the sand, the spinifex and the red earth are dauntingly beautiful.

Another man, another journey

Wednesday 10 December. Another Brit, Howard Holdsworth, had also been bitten by the travel bug. He was from Halifax, Yorkshire and an unlikely mix of businessman and free spirit. He had studied commerce at Harrow but was much more passionate about travelling. He had travelled in Europe, the Americas and Africa and now it was Down Under's turn. Staying with friends in Broome in north-west Western Australia, he decided to head north a little way in a hired jeep and camp in a nature reserve there.

The only trouble was, there weren't many sign posts in that part of the country. He missed the turn-off and ended up at Menari, 70 kilometres north of Broome. And his travel plans went out the window when he got bogged on the deserted beach there. He tried to dig himself out but had no luck. So he decided to stay put. He set up camp for the night in a mangrove forest. As darkness fell, he couldn't just sense the presence of crocodiles in a nearby creek, he could see the reflection of their eyes. And he knew they could see him.

Footprints walking away from the car

Thursday 11 December. Thomas Sykes was driving through an extraordinary landscape. Strangely dramatic and deadly at the same time. He was about 60 kilometres east of Punmu when he got bogged in the desert sands. If he had taken a satellite phone with him, he could have called for help. If he had hired an emergency beacon, he could have signalled that he was in difficulty. If he had stayed put, he would have been found and everything would have been rosy. But when contractors working in the area came upon the vehicle later that afternoon, he was nowhere to be found. All they saw were footprints walking away from the car.

The first rule of survival in the Outback is very simple: stay with your car. Walking for help is not an option. It's not just a stroll up the road; it's staggering though merciless 42°C heat. Distance is on a vast scale here, totally different to the rolling green countryside of the UK. When you find an empty car in town, no-one bats an eyelid. But when you come across an empty vehicle in the Outback, it takes on an ominous significance. And locals tend to fear the worst.

When the workers found Thomas Sykes' abandoned vehicle, they rang police and began a preliminary search themselves. Aboriginal trackers followed his footsteps along the gravel, back towards Punmu. But one of those fairly frequent sandstorms blew up, covering his tracks and making the search pretty well impossible.

Meanwhile, Howard Holdsworth knew that remaining with his vehicle was his best chance of survival. It could provide shelter. It was more easily seen from the air than a tiny figure somewhere out in the middle of nowhere. He didn't take much convincing to stay put: by ten o'clock in the morning, it had already hit 45°C. He had clean water with him but it wasn't going to last forever. He knew if help didn't arrive in the next day or so, he would have to make a difficult decision: stay or go. It would be suicide to attempt the walk back to Broome in the heat of the day, so he thought about walking at night. But it was too early to make that decision just yet.

SOS in the sand

Howard spent a second night in the same spot. He was not desperate but he was scared. He conserved energy by resting during the day and trying to dig the vehicle out at night. He reckons he must have shifted tons of sand.

Then he had a nifty idea worthy of a modern-day Robinson Crusoe. With his feet, he sketched out SOS in giant letters in the sand. Not just anywhere. In the damp sand, below the high water mark on the beach, so that anyone who saw it from the air would know that it had been written recently. He re-wrote the letters the next morning after the high tide washed them away.

He didn't know it, but Customs and Coastwatch do regular aerial patrols along that stretch of coastline. It just so happened that a member of the crew was looking through binoculars when the plane passed overhead. SOS written in the sand from 500 feet at 140 knots is hard to see. But see it they did during a low-level pass. They did a return sweep and spotted Howard's vehicle about one kilometre inland at a point called Cape Bertholet. Howard stood on the beach, frantically waving a piece of cloth. The plane banked its wings. They were signalling to him. He felt blessed relief as well he might. No-one knew he was missing. He'd told his friends he'd be back on Saturday. Fortunately for him, it was only the second time in nine years that the coastal patrol had spotted an individual by sheer chance.

On Friday 12 December, the search for Thomas Sykes was well and truly underway by first light. The assumption was that he had back-tracked, heading in the direction of Punmu and it proved true. He was found just under five kilometres from the settlement, collapsed by the side of the road. He had walked an incredible 40 kilometres in temperatures in excess of 40°C. He was severely dehydrated: most of the water he had was back in his four-wheel drive. He was alive and able to talk but slipping in and out of consciousness.

A toss of the coin

After Howard Holdsworth was rescued he described the feeling of having to make a life and death decision. 'I had to pause and think about death,' he said. 'I had to face the fact that I was in a situation where I could make one or two right decisions and 100 wrong ones. It's a deadly environment and the heat is ferocious. I could have died if I'd stayed with the vehicle and died if I'd left it. It was 50-50, a toss of the coin …'

A toss of the coin. The coin fell on the right side for Howard Holdsworth but not for Thomas Sykes. The Aboriginal trackers along with a nurse rushed Sykes to Punmu's medical clinic but his condition worsened. He lapsed into final unconsciousness and resuscitation failed. His rescuers were distraught. He had got to within five kilometres of help. He had been found, comforted, given medical care and brought back to safety. But he didn't make it. Shortly after reaching Punmu, Thomas Sykes died.

MISSING

THE MAN WHO JUST WANTED TO BE ALONE

Name:	**Robert Bogucki**
Age:	**33 years old**
Nationality:	**American**
Incident:	**Missing**
When:	**Set out 12 July 1999; reported missing 26 July 1999; found 23 August 1999**
Where:	**Great Sandy Desert, Western Australia**
Outcome:	**Non-fatal**

Is this the triumphant story of a man found after walking 400 kilometres through the Great Sandy Desert? Or is it the tale of wasted police resources and a madman who went off into the wilderness on a path of spiritual enlightenment and didn't want to be found? Robert Bogucki's survival for 42 days in the Outback is a great feat of human endurance. And the whole saga of the US search team coming to WA under the command of a cigar-smoking Lieutenant Colonel is entertaining stuff. The TV crew who went over the line in their desperate quest for an 'exclusive' adds a nice touch of farce. All in all, Robert Bogucki's story has it all: conflict, endurance, quiet contentment, fear and a touch of craziness too.

The bike

It all started with a bicycle. On 26 July 1999, some tourists in north-western Australia found an old blue bike and some camping gear on a remote dirt track about 50 kilometres from the Sandfire road-house, about the only stopover for travellers heading north to Broome. It rang alarm bells. The cyclist was probably disorientated, dehydrated and possibly dead. A major search began, involving Broome police, dozens of personnel, Aboriginal trackers and other volunteers. The trouble was, the owner of the bicycle wasn't in trouble at all.

The bike belonged to Robert Bogucki, firefighter and adventurer from the icy lands of Alaska. He'd flown into Sydney in early 1999 and cycled thousands of kilometres across the country, eventually arriving in the rugged north-west of Western Australia. It's tough country with dense scrub and spiky spinifex stretching as far as the eye can see. Robert Bogucki was here for a purpose. In early July, he rang his long-time girlfriend, Janet North, in Texas, discussed his intentions and promised to ring her by 22 August. In the last week of July, he stopped in at the Sandfire road-house. He wrote a postcard to his parents also telling them of his plan. And this was it: he would cross the Great Sandy Desert and end up at Fitzroy Crossing about 600 kilometres away, no mean feat.

Robert set out on his bike. He cycled up the Great Northern Highway and turned east onto the Pegasus Track. Two days down the track, he realised it was easier to walk than to cycle, so he abandoned his bike. When his bike was found, the search team began looking in the immediate vicinity, expecting to find a desperate thirst-crazed cyclist. Little did they know that the object of their search was striding confidently across the desert sands with a two-week, 100-kilometre headstart.

Meanwhile, Broome police had found a clue in the lining of a jacket that had been abandoned with the bike. It was a receipt for a night's accommodation in Tasmania, signed Robert Bogucki, Fairbanks, Alaska. At least they knew who they were looking for. Police contacted Janet North who told them Robert may well have left the bike behind because it was slowing him down. Which, as it happens, was exactly the case.

After two weeks without finding a trace of the 'missing' man, the search was abandoned with locals fearing the worst. Janet flew in for the final stages of the search. She threw in a new dynamic by revealing that it was possible Robert was deliberately avoiding the search party because he was on a personal quest to test his endurance and on a path of 'spiritual enlightenment'. Police didn't quite know what to make of this, other than to say that such a quest might cost him his life.

All this time, Robert Bogucki had no inkling of the trouble his old blue bicycle had caused. He had no idea that there was a major search and rescue operation underway. He had found a place of absolute solitude, somewhere free from distractions, pressures, noise and all the madness of urban life. He had found a sand ridge with a beautiful view of the desert. There were several shady hollows so that he could move into the shade at different times of the day while the sun moved across the sky. He stayed there for one week.

And then? 'At the end of the week I just felt inspired that it was time to keep going,' he said. 'I figured it was going to take another two weeks to get to the road-house near the Fitzroy River. When the eighth day came around it felt right to leave. I felt really strong at that point.' (*The West Australian Big Weekend*, p. 2, 4 September 1999).

US search team

Meanwhile, Bogucki's California-based parents were unimpressed by the notion that their son was playing a game of cat and mouse with police. Ray Bogucki—a retired lawyer—and his wife Betty weren't ones to beat around the bush. Once the two-week search was abandoned, they approached the US government for help. The US State Department linked them up with a Special Response Group run by a 49-year-old retired US Army Lieutenant Colonel by the name of Garrison St Clair. Together, they organised a $40, 000+ expedition funded by Robert's parents with a little help from the US Government and the airline that flew them to Australia.

And so, ten days after the first search was abandoned, the Americans rolled into town. Garrison St Clair led a team of eight with three tracker dogs and dog handlers. The Australian Government waived the usual quarantine ruling so the dogs could get going ASAP. But things were held up a little when it was discovered the pooches needed custom-made leather shoes to protect their paws from the scratchy spinifex.

Soon personnel and dogs were ready to go. Broome police were understandably wary of the new arrivals. There was quite possibly a hint of professional jealousy, but they were also entirely reasonable in questioning whether the US volunteers could cope with the extreme desert conditions. The Americans quickly showed that they had all the necessary survival skills. They were still hoping to find Robert Bogucki alive, but realistically it was more likely that they would find a corpse.

Thursday 19 August. The US trackers set off on a five-day operation with six local volunteers and a police adviser. They arrived at their base camp, 228 kilometres SE of Broome. Almost immediately, one of the sniffer dogs picked up Robert Bogucki's scent. They were amazed to find footprints in the sand on the McLarty Track, a rarely used trail and one of three possible routes. It was basically sheer good fortune that they had picked the right one.

The footprints were only a few days old which led them to believe that they were less than three days behind their pursuit. It seemed that he was heading for the Edgar Ranges and fresh water.

The next day, their optimism was offset by the difficult conditions: heat, dense scrub, spinifex. Even the tracker dogs were overcome with exhaustion. But then they found a second set of footprints. Against the odds, it seemed that Robert Bogucki was indeed alive and well and within reach. Roberts's parents were advised that things looked hopeful. The prints showed Robert was still going well. His stride was lengthy and he seemed to be walking barefoot on the sand and wearing shoes on the rougher ground. They were not the footprints of someone sick or desperately fatigued. It was clear to everyone that here was a man with very well-honed survival skills.

Another positive sighting occurred two days later on Sunday 22 August when an abandoned pile of gear was found just two kilometres from base camp. Clothes, two hats, water bottle, chocolate wrappers and a Bible. They were closing in on him.

The great day came on Monday 23 August. Robert Bogucki was spotted at 8.30am, walking in a deep gorge 225 kilometres SE of Broome.

Wearing a filthy T-shirt and army pants, he was carrying a clean white T-shirt given to him by his girlfriend, to look respectable in case he made it to a road and had to hitchhike. He had discarded the stuff the search team had found the day before because he was too weak to carry it all. But he still had his water bottle—filled with unappetising but life-sustaining eucalypt tea—his passport and his return ticket to Alaska. Clearly, this was a man who had no intention of dying in the desert far from home. He was weak, tired, hungry and 27 kilograms lighter then when he had set out on his marathon stint, but apart from a few minor cuts on his feet and back, he was in surprisingly good health. Ironically he wasn't found by the US team or Broome police but by a helicopter TV camera crew from Channel Nine.

The media

Weird allegations surrounded Channel Nine's handling of the Robert Bogucki rescue. A leaked video tape showed them asking him to walk for the camera—hadn't he done enough?—and not giving him any water for more than 15 minutes. They also delayed his flight to hospital when he was sick in the helicopter after eating a banana they had given him. They filmed him being sick and then used the footage as if it was footage of him being found. Police also investigated claims that authorities were not informed that he had been found for up to 40 minutes while Channel Nine got its interview.

To recuperate and avoid further media debacles, Robert Bogucki and Janet North took up a kind offer of hospitality from Sergeant Geoff Fuller, who had led the original search. They stayed at his home in Broome for several days. Robert Bogucki had incited a lot of public interest and received many letters via the Broome police, many of which were censored by the police. Many of them showed no sympathy for the survival-savvy Alaskan, calling him 'that totally deranged American' and worse (*The Australian*, p. 7, 4 September 1999). Robert Bogucki was upset by the content of some of the letters and was defended by Sergeant

Fuller who said that Robert was now aware of the mammoth search effort made to find him and was concerned about the resources used. He didn't deserve to cop such abuse because, most of all, he was 'a lovely bloke' (ibid).

On 3 September, Robert Bogucki and Janet North caught a bus to Alice Springs. From there they visited Uluru, then Sydney and finally back to the USA and home.

What are we to make of Robert Bogucki? He had set off on a quest that many would find hard to understand. He was fit, survival-savvy and had told his family of his plans. He dug for water and then covered up the holes, not wanting any creatures to fall in and become trapped. He carried his empty tuna tin and chocolate wrappers with him, not wanting to leave rubbish behind. These are not the signs of an irresponsible man. He didn't ask for help—it's possible he didn't need help—but towards the end he was quite happy to be 'saved'. After all, for the final two weeks of his adventure he had eaten nothing and his strength was waning. He had used rocks to spell out HELP on top of a gorge, but no-one saw it. Incredible endurance? Definitely. Unfathomable? To some. Whatever the case, it's unlikely he'll try it again. As he is reported to have said to his rescuers, 'I'm done with walking'. (*The Sydney Morning Herald*, p. 1, 24 August 1999).

DINGO

THE BABY,
THE DINGO AND THE MURDER TRIAL

Name:	**Azaria Chamberlain**
Age:	**9½ weeks old**
Nationality:	**Australian**
Incident:	**Dingo attack**
When:	**17 August 1980**
Where:	**Uluru, Northern Territory**
Outcome:	**Fatal**

The simplest explanation is usually the best. But that's not what the Australian public wanted from Michael and Lindy Chamberlain. They wanted a bizarre, twisted account of what happened on the night of 17 August 1980. They wanted something gruesome, evidence of some weirdo cultish sacrifice; they wanted a whiff of scandal. Michael was a pastor, awkward and well-meaning; Lindy was sharper, practical, more assertive. The first journalist to sniff out the story didn't like them so they were off to a bad start. Was Azaria a love child? Did they take a different baby on holiday with them, having done away with her earlier? Was she retarded? Did her name mean Sacrifice in the Wilderness? The answers are as follows: no, no, no and no.

The ongoing saga

The story of Azaria Chamberlain is a well-documented saga that has stretched on for over 25 years. Legal precedents, three inquests, tainted evidence, findings quashed, battles for compensation, divorce, strange sightings of a grown-up 'Azaria', it's all there. As well as one still unidentified dingo. These days dingos are recognised as capable of fatal attack, especially so since the death of young Clinton Gage at Fraser Island in 2001. There have been numerous reports of dingos stealthily padding around campsites and into hotel rooms and fixating on young children (See 'The Dingos That Attack Children', in chapter 5).

If evidence of dingos' capacity to kill was taken more seriously in 1980, perhaps Lindy's story would have been believed. If dingo behaviour had been understood as more wolf-like than dog-like, perhaps she would have been believed. If Lindy had cried on camera, gone public with her private grief, played a part rather than been herself, perhaps she would have been believed. Through the Chamberlains' protracted legal battle to have their names cleared, it's hard to cut through all the rigmarole and see this story for what it is and what it was: an Aussie family on a camping trip.

They set out from Mt Isa on holidays, Mum, Dad and three kids. Two boys, aged six and four, and a little baby girl. First stop was Tennant Creek, where they had a look around, and then the Devil's Marbles where they camped that night. The next day they travelled on to Alice Springs where they camped at Heavitree Gap. The next day they got the petrol pump fixed and stayed another night in Alice. There was a rodeo in town and it was a little too noisy and chaotic, so they headed off at lunchtime to Uluru, or Ayer's Rock as it was known then. They were hoping to get there to see it at sunset, but they missed it. The next morning, they did some scooting round The Rock, taking photos, doing things families do on holidays. One innocent photograph of Lindy holding up little Azaria as if she is standing would remain an image of a precious life lost.

The family stopped at an ancient rock formation known on the tourist circuit as 'The Cave of Fertility'. 'Is that your dog?' Lindy reportedly asked a holiday-maker from Geraldton, Western Australia, who was busy lining up his camera for another shot. She pointed to an animal standing atop a boulder only a couple of metres from them. 'No,' he answered, 'That's a dingo.'

The campsite

The Chamberlain family returned to the campsite just on sunset. Lindy put their younger son, Reagan, to bed. While Michael busied himself with the cooking and their older boy, Aidan, waited around for something to eat, Lindy held her baby and chatted with the neighbouring campers, Sally and Greg Lowe from Tasmania. Not much later, Sally went to take some scraps over to the garbage bins. On the way back, she had a strange feeling she was being followed. She looked back and there was a dingo, padding along silently behind her. She quickened her pace back to the campfire. The dingo disappeared.

The Whittackers, another family of campers that night, had their camp table set up for washing-up with a gas lantern that cast a soft circle of light on the ground. They noticed movement at the edge of the arc of light. It was a dingo, stealthily padding around the very edge of the light and then disappearing in the direction of the barbecues.

Michael and Aidan were hunting for a mouse by torchlight when Michael saw a dingo and threw it a piece of bread. Lindy told him it was a silly thing to do. Father and son returned to their mouse hunt. Michael saw the mouse and pointed it out, but the dingo pounced. No more mouse.

Baby Azaria fell asleep in Lindy's arms, so Lindy and Aidan took her to the tent to bed. They raced back from the tent to the barbecues ten minutes later in a pseudo 'race', with Lindy coming a close second. Lindy had a can opener and a tin of baked beans which she began to heat up for her little boy. Another camper nearby sat reading a book about wildlife. A sound made her look up. The growl of a dog. It had come from the direction of the Chamberlain's tent. Sally Lowe heard the baby cry, a sharp, incomplete sound. Michael and Aidan heard it too. Lindy headed back to the tent, surprised that the baby had stirred. After all, she had been fast asleep.

Lindy burst out with her famous cry, 'My God. My God. The dingo's got my baby.' And it all escalated completely out of control.

The inquest

20 February 1981. The inquest was led by Denis Barritt who concluded, 'I doth find that Azaria Chantel Loren Chamberlain, a child then of nine weeks of age and formerly of Mt Isa, Queensland, met her death when attacked by a wild dingo whilst asleep in her family's tent at the top camping area, Ayers Rock, shortly after eight pm on 17 August 1980.'

Denis Barritt felt compelled to make a public apology to the Chamberlains: 'To you, Pastor and Mrs Chamberlain, and through you Aidan and Reagan, may I extend my deepest sympathy. You have not only suffered the loss of your beloved child in the most tragic circumstances, but you have all been subjected to months of innuendoes, suspicion, and probably the most malicious gossip ever witnessed in this country …'

Denis Barritt was critical of investigations, particularly the Forensic Science Section of the Northern Territory Police Force. Some of his findings and recommendations appear not to have gone down at all well in some circles. From this point, there seems to have been a decided shift, a desire among some for pay back for what the inquest had uncovered. It seems that there were some all too willing to 'get' Lindy, to make her pay for the fact that they had been hauled over the coals.

And so, soon after the inquest, a new police taskforce was set up code named Operation Ochre. On 27 May they sent Azaria's clothing to Adelaide for more forensic tests. On 20 September the police turned up on the Chamberlains' doorstep with a search warrant and news that fresh scientific evidence had turned up; but when asked what the new evidence was, they said they'd search first and answer questions later. The second inquest, run by a different Coroner, led to Lindy Chamberlain being committed to stand trial for the murder of her daughter and Michael Chamberlain charged as an accessory after the fact.

A motiveless murder

13 September 1982. The trial began. The Crown case was that Azaria Chamberlain was murdered by her mother; and they set out to prove this using scientific evidence about the baby's clothes. They did not attempt to suggest any reason or motive for the killing, a puzzling omission. If you piece together their arguments and suppositions, you end up with a scenario something like this:

At some time between 8-9pm on the night of 17 August 1980, Lindy Chamberlain must have:

- transformed—for reasons unknown—into a homicidal maniac
- cut her baby's throat with a pair of scissors
- hidden the body in the car in her husband's camera bag
- washed her hands and clothes to remove all trace of baby blood
- returned to the campsite, chatting to campers with a bundle in her arms that she had cunningly made to look like a real baby
- went to the tent with her son and pretended to put 'the baby' to bed
- returned to the campsite with her son, a can opener and a tin of baked beans, acting as if nothing at all had happened
- fortuitously taken the opportunity to put on a big charade that a dingo had taken her baby when other campers—whom she had only met that evening—heard a dog's growl
- and finally, disposed of her baby's body later (with Michael's help) when the whole campsite was out looking for a dingo.

On 29 October 1982, in a shocking verdict, Lindy Chamberlain was found guilty of murder and sentenced to life imprisonment. Michael Chamberlain was found guilty of being an accessory after the fact and was given an 18-month suspended sentence.

Overturning the evidence

The assertion that baby Azaria's blanket had been cut with scissors was later disproved: it had in fact been eaten by wool-moths. Azaria's clothes and bedding had been sent to Adelaide for examination by forensic biologists, but they had not been informed that animal hairs had first been removed in Darwin. The photograph of the position and arrangement of Azaria's clothing when first discovered proved to be false; the policeman who took the photo had picked the clothes up and then attempted to recreate what he had found.

No-one seriously considered that a dingo could take a baby from its jumpsuit except people who understood dingo behaviour, but their evidence was not called for. A camper had found an imprint of knitted fabric on the dunes that night, but it had not been photographed or considered important. 'Blood' on the passenger foot-well in the Chamberlain's car—crudely known as 'the arterial spray'—turned out to be Dufix 1081, a sound-deadening compound used in Torana LX SLs. 'Foetal blood' supposedly on the car floor was nothing more than an old milkshake spill. There were tests done to find saliva on the baby's jumpsuit but it had been raining the night before it was found; and further, Lindy claimed and continued to claim that Azaria had been wearing a matinee jacket.

Lindy's claim was finally vindicated. Azaria had been wearing a matinee jacket, and it was discovered in a most bizarre fashion (See 'The Man Who Fell Off Uluru', this chapter). The discovery explained why Azaria's jumpsuit did not have saliva on it, and explained the knitted fabric impressions that had been found in the sand on the night she disappeared.

7 February 1986. The acting editor of Darwin's *The Northern Territory News* became fed up with not being given the full story from the Northern Territory Government. He set up a front-page story to expose the fact that important information about the Chamberlain case was not being released to the public. The story he chose exposed the faulty testing procedure used to 'prove' that the blood in the Chamberlains' car was foetal blood. He sent off a copy of his proposed lead story to the Northern Territory Attorney-General's press secretary and what followed was rather interesting. There was an emergency meeting of Cabinet. And

at midday—just before the presses rolled—he received a phone call from the Chief Minister of the Northern Territory himself with a big scoop: they were releasing Lindy Chamberlain.

In September 1988, the Supreme Court quashed all convictions and found the Chamberlains innocent. In May 1992, Michael Chamberlain received $400,000 compensation; Lindy $900,000. Their legal fees totalled much more than that, somewhere up around $5 million.

The legacy

It's hard to imagine being maligned and forced to recount agonising memories over and over again. It's impossible to understand what Michael and Lindy Chamberlain went through. And it's distressing to imagine the effects that this unbelievable trial had on the Chamberlains, their family and the families who were camping at Uluru that night. Eye-witnesses at the campsite, rangers and trackers who followed the dingo prints were of one mind: a dingo had taken baby Azaria from her family's tent. It was only those who weren't there that night who questioned Lindy and Michael Chamberlain's story. By twisting standard judicial procedure and passing off inaccurate forensic testing as scientific fact, they managed to change the story of a family on a camping holiday into something very different.

FATAL FALL

Uluru is hard to describe and even harder to explain. To the *Anangu* (the Pitjantjatjara and Yankunytjatjara people), parts of it are sacred; to white Australians it is something of an icon; to overseas visitors it is an extraordinary tourist attraction or maybe a challenge to climb. Anyone who has laid eyes on Uluru will tell you that it has an inherent fascination. From a distance, it looks smooth but it's not at all. If you walk round the base—a fascinating nine kilometre level walk—you will see caves, indentations, deep shadows and a sublime rich rust-red colour in a myriad of patterns, textures and forms.

To the *Anangu,* these features are related to the journeys of ancestral beings across the landscape and together they form a collection of stories known as Tjukurpa. The *Anangu* do not like people to climb Uluru. They respectfully request that visitors do not climb for two reasons. One, 'The Climb' criss-crosses part of an ancient ancestral path; and two, it is very distressing to them, as custodians of The Rock, when someone dies. Die they do and continue to climb they do, but in gradually decreasing numbers.

THE MAN WHO FELL OFF ULURU

Name:	**David Brett**
Age:	**31 years old**
Nationality:	**British**
Incident:	**Falling off Uluru**
When:	**26 January 1986**
Where:	**Northern Territory**
Outcome:	**Fatal**

About 400,000 or so tourists come to Uluru each year; less than half of them attempt 'The Climb'. The current estimate is that roughly one person a month dies either directly or indirectly as a result of climbing Uluru. It might be a heart attack brought on by heat stroke, it might be a fatal fall or it may be a heart attack one or two days later in the comfort of a hotel room. Strangely, the names of people who plunge to their deaths from Uluru are not familiar to most Australians. Shark attack victims have their names splashed across the front page of daily papers. Tourists who drown get great media coverage. But if you plunge to your death at Uluru, you won't rate much of a mention. One such victim's name is hardly well-known, but when he fell to his death on Australia Day in 1986 he set in place an unbelievable chain of events that would end with the release of a (wrongly) convicted murderer from her prison cell. The climber's name was David Brett; the prisoner was Lindy Chamberlain. This is their story.

An interest in mysticism

David Brett was someone driven to achieve one goal, to climb Uluru for personal and spiritual reasons. David was from Harley in Kent and had spent about four years in Australia where he became interested in mysticism and the occult. He then returned home to the UK before returning to Australia, specifically Central Australia.

David arrived at Uluru in the middle of summer. The day was abominably hot, so he waited until just before sunset to set out on his quest, taking a small backpack with him. He didn't stick to the marked path: a group of tourists leaving at the end of the day saw his small figure high above them, climbing up the western side of The Rock; a steep, difficult climb in the fading light.

Some say David Brett was mentally ill. Others say God had told him to climb Uluru where he was to be transported into heaven. Whatever the case, David fell about 46 metres to his death. Police found his body eight days later in an area riddled with dingo lairs. It was also the area where a camper had found Azaria Chamberlain's clothes six years before (See 'The Baby, the Dingo and the Murder Trial', this chapter).

The area was cordoned off. The corpse was badly decomposed and had been attacked by dingos; it was missing an arm and part of a leg. Perhaps a thorough search of the area would yield some body parts. David's T-shirt, shorts and a kerchief were all scattered about, presumably because a dingo had been rummaging through his backpack. But there was something else: a filthy bundle that had originally been white, lying on the ground encrusted with dirt. It was a baby's knitted matinee jacket.

Convictions quashed

The Chamberlains' solicitor was tipped off that it had been found. A few days later, it was taken to Lindy Chamberlain in Berrimah Jail. She instantly identified it as Azaria's jacket, and forensically this was shown to be the case. This was a crucial turning point in the Chamberlain saga. The prosecution hadn't believed there ever was a jacket, but Lindy had always insisted there was. The jacket explained why there was no dingo saliva on Azaria's jumpsuit and it explained the knitted pattern found in an indentation in the sand the night Azaria disappeared. The jacket was the key to Lindy Chamberlain's innocence. She was released from prison. A 14-month long Royal Commission into the investigation cleared the Chamberlains of any wrong-doing. More than a year later, the Court of Criminal Appeal quashed their convictions but they then had to wait four years for compensation.

How incredible that David Brett plunged to his death in that place. How astonishing that his lifeless body set in motion such a chain of events. He had played a part in something much bigger than himself. As we all do.

Did you know?

In a classic case of being unprepared and unaware, a very embarrassed Irish man and his daughter had to be airlifted from Uluru in 2006. They had set off to climb The Rock wearing plastic sandals which began to virtually melt because of the heat. Rangers closed the climb at 8am that day because it was going to be a scorcher; but by that time the dynamic duo was already about 100 metres up. The 38-year-old man's feet became so blistered that he took off his sandals and attempted to keep climbing with his shirt tied around his sore feet. But this didn't last long. Soon he was in agony; his feet were badly cut with extreme blistering and he was suffering from dehydration. His 13-year-old daughter too was feeling the full effects of the heat; she was having trouble breathing.

A tour operator noticed the pair in distress and raised the alarm. A ranger responded, climbing The Rock at the worst possible time of day. He reached the distressed pair in the extreme heat of the midday sun and guided them to one of four spots on the rock where a helicopter could land. When the chopper arrived with medical help, the man was put on a drip and treated for his severe blisters; the ranger was later taken to hospital with an injured leg. The family were pathetically grateful and offered to pay the $600 it cost for the helicopter rescue.

10.
Sky

The sky is the final frontier. The Australian sky is bright blue with not a hint of depressing grey haze; it's not surprising that sometimes we yearn to be more than earthbound. Here are stories of people who look to the skies for excitement, enjoyment or liberty. The first is a hot-air balloon tragedy in Central Australia when 13 people died; the second is about a well-known BASE jumper from Iceland who comes to Australia and plunges to his death—ironically—in a parachute. And finally, there's the miraculous account of a paraglider who gets sucked up into a storm cell, slips into unconsciousness, flies higher than Mount Everest and then finds her way back down to earth, astonished, laughing and alive.

HOT-AIR BALLOON

THE BALLOON
THAT PLUMMETED TO EARTH

Name:	**Anthony Fraser (pilot)**
Age:	24 years old
Nationality:	Australian
Incident:	Hot-air balloon
When:	13 August 1989
Where:	Alice Springs, Northern Territory
Outcome:	**Fatal**

The names of the twelve passengers who also died:

Name:	**Garry Dover**
Age:	34 years old
Name:	**Jennifer Dover**
Age:	34 years old
Name:	**Daniel Fitzgibbon**
Age:	68 years old
Name:	**Maurie Longden**
Age:	51 years old
Name:	**Lawrence Murphy**
Age:	29 years old
Name:	**Veronica Murphy**
Age:	27 years old
Nationality:	All from Victoria, Australia
Name:	**Daphne Nell Overton**
Age:	66 years old
Name:	**Belinda Louise Reid**
Age:	30 years old

Name:	**Claire Taylor**
Age:	**57 years old**
Nationality:	**All from NSW, Australia**
Name:	**Rosemary Margaret Smith**
Age:	**27 years old**
Nationality:	**from South Australia**
Name:	**Priben Jacobsonen**
Age:	**26 years old**
Nationality:	**Danish**
Name:	**Unnamed**
Nationality:	**Italian**

This is the story of the worst hot-air balloon accident in the world to date. Thirteen people lost their lives when a hot-air balloon at 1000 metres clipped the basket of the balloon above. It's a tragedy with many layers. It's the story of lives cut short in a shocking event: a young honeymooning couple, a father of ten, these were just three of the ordinary holiday-makers who never came home. It's the story of the young pilot who, on that very day, was on the verge of qualifying for his chief pilot's licence. And it's a story told through eyewitnesses, joyriding on other balloons at the time, who experienced at first-hand how powerless we are in the face of horror. In a car accident, you can pull victims from the wreckage; if someone is bitten by a snake, you can apply a tourniquet. But when a balloon falls out of the sky, all you can do is watch …

From the air

In Australia, flying is a necessity. In the Outback, mail is delivered by plane, food supplies come in by plane, the Royal Flying Doctor Service provides medical aid and even Members of Parliament fly between their constituents because there's just too much distance between them. It's not surprising that one of the best ways to experience the interior of

Australia is from the air. And it's not surprising that at Alice Springs, there's a number of companies happy to take your $200+ and give you a thrilling 30-minute dawn hot-air balloon experience which usually ends with a celebratory champagne breakfast in a suitably scenic Outback spot.

The sight of enormous six-storey hot-air balloons sailing over Alice Springs at dawn is a magnificent sight: the vivid stripes of the balloons, the splendour of the landscape below as they sail up to 1000 metres. From up here, you can see vast stretches of red sand dotted with spinifex and mulga, red kangaroos and wallabies lolloping around at the start of their day. From up here, you can sense the isolation of this extraordinary part of Australia. But then you look around, you're with twelve others in a hot-air balloon adrift in the brilliant blue sky. It's a stunning morning and all's right with the world.

One Sunday, a bus-load of tourists pulled up at the hot-air balloon launch site at Santa Teresa Mission Road, about 25 kilometres SE of Alice Springs. The weather that morning was bright and still, perfect conditions for a scenic flight. Four big beautiful balloons were set to take off together, which is not at all unusual. Hundred of balloons can be launched together with no ill effects. Balloons in flight do bump into each other occasionally, again usually with no bad consequences. That is, until this particular morning.

The six-storey maroon and yellow-striped balloon known as *VH-NMS* had pilot Anthony Fraser at the helm. Anthony was a passionate canoeist, abseiler, rock climber and balloon pilot. He had arrived in Alice Springs with his girlfriend Laura only the month before. He was here to have a full-on working holiday before returning to Melbourne to run 'Go Wild Ballooning' with his brother Mark. This was a big day for Anthony: it was the day he would notch up the required 150 hours flying time to qualify for a chief pilot's licence.

The four balloons lifted into the air and travelled together, a majestic sight against the backdrop of sky. Anthony's balloon had twelve passengers on board. There were six men and six women, six from Victoria, three from NSW; a woman from South Australia, a man from Denmark and another man from Italy. Irene Fielder, a German tourist taking her first balloon ride ever in a nearby balloon, noticed that the maroon and yellow balloon was rising quite fast, directly under another balloon.

Collision

The balloon was up to about 1000 metres when it clipped the basket, or gondola, of the balloon above. A New Zealand tourist in the top balloon reported afterwards that it had appeared so suddenly that no one had seen it coming. It's also alleged that, later, the pilot of the top balloon commented to one of his passengers that he had not seen the other balloon before they collided (Australian Transport Safety Bureau, Aircraft Occurrence Report No. 198900820, p. 2, 1989).

There was a ripping sound and the sound of rushing air as the top of the balloon was slashed open. The gondola began to shake. Those in the top balloon screamed, but there was no sound from below. The ripped balloon slowly began to move away. There was something disturbing about its painfully slow-motion movement. Even though it was Irene Fielder's debut ride, she knew something was wrong.

7.08am. A mayday call went out to Alice Springs Air Traffic Control. A light plane and helicopter immediately took off; back-up vehicles headed out as support crews for the other balloons. The pilot of the top balloon calmed his passengers and sought an emergency landing site.

In the disabled balloon, Anthony Fraser frantically blasted hot air into the misshapen folds of fabric. 'There didn't seem to be much panic,' Irene Fielder reported, 'They must have been hoping everything would be all right.' (*The Daily Mirror*, p. 4, 14 August, 1989). But then eyewitnesses watched in horror as the stricken balloon began its descent.

The fall

At first, its movement was fairly slow. It fell, listlessly, deflating as it went. But at 200 metres, it lost all shape and plummeted to earth. In their last moments the passengers clung to each other, locking arms together.

Ken Watts who was piloting another balloon nearby saw the death fall. To him and many others watching, time seemed to stand still as the balloon crashed to the ground. There was a sense of being separate, merely an onlooker frozen in time. 'When you see something as horrific as that was,' he said, 'it seemed to take an eternity but it might have been a very short space of time.' The fall didn't take an eternity, it lasted 51 seconds.

A cloud of dust burst up from the ground. The wicker basket split apart on impact. The balloon was ripped to shreds, like streamers flapping limply at the end of a carnival. Clothing, shoes and hats were strewn around the open scrub land. Police and paramedics found ten bodies in the basket with their arms locked tightly around each other. Three bodies had been tossed out on impact.

It was the worst balloon fatality to date. So many lives were affected in direct and indirect ways. The bus driver of a 30-day camping tour had to go the morgue to identify the bodies of seven passengers on his tour. Those on the tour group who had formed strong friendships with the deceased were devastated. Eyewitnesses were left with re-living the moment; and feeling the trauma and guilt associated with knowing that they were there and could do nothing. But sadly, most of all, Danish, Italian and interstate police began the thankless task of knocking on relatives' doors with tragic news. And the families of the dead were left only with memories.

Puzzling cause

It is highly unusual for a pilot to lose control of a balloon even if it is damaged in flight; and balloons that are airworthy and property maintained should not malfunction. An official record of the crash states, 'The pilot of an ascending balloon failed to ensure separation from the balloon above … the ascending balloon struck the basket of the above tearing it and causing the velcro rip panel to open' (www.ema.gov.au/ema/emadisasters). This velcro flap cannot be resealed in flight; and once opened, it is possible for a balloon to rapidly lose altitude.

A further clue comes from Hansard (p. 41, 28 June 1996): 'Thirteen people died when one of the balloons descended onto the other, puncturing it and sending it into a fatal 600 metre free fall ... the pilot (who) was found by the subsequent inquest into the accident to have been grossly negligent in allowing his balloon to descend upon the other ...'

What is known is that the two pilots were not in radio contact with each other; the top balloon was not fitted with a mandatory instrument package for reading altitude and vertical movement; and the Operations Manual clearly stated: 'FORMATION FLIGHT: When two or more balloons are flying together the upper balloon must give way ...' (ATSB, Aircraft Occurrence Report No. 198900820, p. 3).

PARACHUTE

THE BASE JUMPER WHO DIED PARACHUTING

Name:	**Benjamin Arnason aka 'Benni the Ice Man'**
Age:	**27 years old**
Nationality:	**Icelandic**
Incident:	**Parachute jump**
When:	**7 January 2007**
Where:	**Bonalbo, NSW**
Outcome:	**Fatal**

This is the story of a man from Iceland who loved testing himself to his limits. He was an internationally recognised BASE jumper. Given the track record of BASE jumping, he could have died anywhere: in Iceland, in Norway, in France. It just happens that he died in Australia. The irony was that he didn't die BASE jumping at all, but doing a parachute jump that went wrong. It's crazy and very sad. But the sadness is somehow lessened by the life-affirming exuberance of those around him. The BASE jumping community is a very strong, supportive group of people but it doesn't play by the rules. They crave the ultimate, they risk their lives, they mourn their dead.

Benni the Ice Man

Benjamin Arnason was one of Iceland's most experienced BASE jumpers. He was well-known on blogs where he was known as 'Benni the Ice Man'. He had strong ties with Australia. Champion Australian skydiver and BASE jumper Chris McDougall had taught Benni how to BASE jump in Norway. Benni was close friends with Anthony Coombes, another one of Australia's most experienced BASE jumpers, who died jumping from a

1100-metre cliff at Trollveggen, also known as the Troll Wall, in Norway in 2006. Benni had come to Australia for an indefinite period for a holiday. And part of his travel plans involved spending Christmas with Anthony Coombes' mother and sister at Goonellabah, near Lismore on the north coast of NSW. After that, Benni planned to see Tasmania and then travel to New Zealand. But first it was time for Superfreak.

Superfreak was in its third year, a big international electronic music festival at the Gorge Station Retreat in Bonalbo, about 100 kilometres west of Lismore. There were 60 live performances of psytrance, electro, funk, house, dub and reggae. And if you don't know what they are, you wouldn't feel comfortable at Superfreak. Also starring were a heap of local and international DJs from Israel, Italy, UK and Denmark, all over three big nights. This was a miniature high-tech Woodstock with cafes, meditation workshops, swimming holes and so-called adventure activities like parachute jumping. Being a keen skydiver and BASE jumper, Benni was more than a little attracted to the adventure side of things. So on the third and final day of the festival, he booked in for a parachute jump.

Benni and another jumper went for the last jump of the night. There had been two earlier jumps, both jumpers landing successfully in the middle of the festival site. Just before 6.45pm, Benni and another jumper prepared to leap out of a helicopter at 2500 feet. The first jumper jumped out. Benni went next, out into the blue.

Police say his parachute did not open until very late in the descent, and even then it did not open according to plan. It appeared that the ropes became tangled and he was already at tree level before he managed to get it open. Once it was open, he was unable to control it.

800 festival-goers watched as Benni crashed into the surrounding trees and then hit the ground heavily. He died instantly from massive head injuries. The other jumper landed safely. Ironically, Benni had joined the Australian Parachute Federation one month earlier.

News travels fast

The day after Benni died, news of his death was already rapidly shooting around the globe thanks to the networks of skydiving websites. Chris McDougall was quick to respond with a heartfelt web-eulogy: 'For those of you who don't know Benni the Ice Man,' Chris wrote, 'he was a legendary dude with a heart of gold with an appetite for fun bigger than anyone I have met. He was a full-on guy that you couldn't help but love. He definitely made the most out of every second. You're a legend Benni, one of a kind and you will definitely be missed.' (*The Sydney Morning Herald*, p. 3, 9 January 2007)

Did you know?

Benni's good friend, Tony Coombes, grew up in northern NSW, lived in Queensland and died BASE jumping in Norway; while Benni grew up in Iceland and travelled across the world to Australia where his life would end. And when he died, his mother was left to mourn two sons: she had already lost another son in a car accident in Iceland.

PARAGLIDING

THE PARAGLIDERS WHO SOARED INTO THE HEAVENS

Name:	**He Zhongpin**
Age:	**42 years old**
Nationality:	**Chinese**
Incident:	**Sucked into storm cell**
When:	**14 February 2007**
Where:	**Manilla, New South Wales**
Outcome:	**Fatal**

Name:	**Ewa Wisnierska**
Age:	**35 years old**
Nationality:	**Polish**
Incident:	**Sucked into storm cell**
When:	**14 February 2007**
Where:	**Manilla, New South Wales**
Outcome:	**Non-fatal**

This is an astonishing story of human survival; a tale of world record-breaking endurance that defies belief. It is the miraculous story of two world-ranked paragliders sucked up into a raging storm cell and rocketed upwards to the cruising altitude of a Boeing 747. One is struck by lightning and dies. The other keeps spinning upwards, unconscious and battered by gigantic hailstones, until she hits a peak altitude of 9946 metres … higher than Mount Everest. Not only that, but she starts dropping, regains consciousness and manages to land safely with agonising frostbite and an extraordinary story to tell.

Routine training run

Ewa Wisnierska is Polish-born and German-based but prefers to be defined as 'European'. Known as 'Birdy' in paragliding circles, Ewa has her own website where she reveals she is a free spirit with top personal goal-setting skills and a killer mental attitude. She has 10 years' experience as a paraglider and is Germany's women's champion. She has consistently ranked first or second in virtually all major European Women's Paragliding Championships.

Ewa was part of a 200-strong group training for the World Paragliding Championships in Manilla—not the bustling Asian city but the smallish country town in north-western NSW about 50 kilometres north of Tamworth and five hours' drive from Sydney.

He Zhongpin, from Beijing, had 10 years' paragliding experience up his sleeve. He was also getting in some practice for the Championships. This is why on Wednesday 14 February, 2007, Ewa and He Zhongpin both went on a routine training run in the run-up to the main events.

1pm. Conditions were ideal. The thermals were smooth and soft, big and wide. Ewa Wisnierska jogged off the lip of Mount Borah and took to the air. Perfect take-off. The flying was beautiful. For an hour or so. A few other international competitors were already in the sky. There were dark clouds to the south but they were nothing to worry about. Ewa estimated she was about 10 kilometres in front of the clouds and there shouldn't be a problem.

2.30pm. Ewa knew she was in trouble. A thunderstorm was looming. The rolling mass of cloud in front of her had turned into two giant storm fronts. She and He Zhongpin were right in the firing line. They may have thought they could fly between the storm cells, but now the storms had merged into one. And they were sucking up everything in their path.

Two paragliders in trouble

Ewa saw a giant cloud coming at her. She tried to fly around it but got sucked up. She tried to spiral against it, once, twice, three times, but she was not strong enough. He Zhongpin was having the same difficulties. At this point his crew lost contact with him. Sadly, they would never regain communication.

3pm. The two paragliders disappeared into the fast-closing gap between the two storm cells. They were nearly 3000 metres above the ground, being sucked up at about 20 metres per second. It was only mid-afternoon but, where they were, it was dark.

Because He Zhongpin's equipment failed due to the extreme cold, it's hard to know exactly what happened to him. But we know that they both climbed higher and higher into the darkness and it started to rain. Hail began to fall and lashed around them. Then the lightning came; it seemed to be coming from every direction. Ewa knew she was in the middle of a thunderstorm but she was powerless against the elements.

He Zhongpin's fate

He Zhongpin was sucked into the same storm cell as Ewa and was catapulted up to 9000 metres. Team mates found his body at 2pm the next day, about 75 kilometres from where he had taken off. Initial reports were that he probably suffocated from lack of oxygen to the brain or froze to death at the extreme altitude. His reserve parachute wasn't used and the batteries of his monitors lost power because of the cold. The preliminary results of the post-mortem carried out the following Monday indicated that he had been struck by lightning.

Ewa's journey

Ewa radioed her team leader at 4000 metres: 'I can't do anything. It's raining and hailing and I'm still climbing. I'm lost.' She knew her chances of survival were virtually zero. And with that thought, she was sucked up higher and higher into the atmosphere. Her sunglasses started to freeze over. She was weak and exhausted. All she could do was climb. The last thing she remembered is making the radio call. Then she blacked out.

Ewa lost consciousness for about 40 minutes while her paraglider flew on uncontrolled, sinking and lifting several times. The temperature was believed to have been around -50°C and her body was beaten by massive hailstones as big as grapefruits. Her track log—a flight trajectory downloaded from her GPS—recorded her top altitude as 9946 metres, over 1000 metres higher than Mount Everest. Few people have ever survived such an experience. Without realising it, she had smashed the world altitude survival record.

Ewa regained consciousness at about 6900 metres. She was freezing cold. Her eyelashes were covered in ice, her harness was full of hail. Everything was frozen. Shaking with shock, and disoriented from lack of oxygen, she had the presence of mind to know that she had to fly out of the cloud ASAP. She scratched her GPS and found she was just under 7000m and still flying. She had no idea how long she had blacked out. She saw her frozen gloves and saw that the handles of her paraglider were up. She was amazed to realise that her glider must have been flying itself.

As she gradually came to, she took in her surroundings. Emerging from the clouds, she felt the sun on the face for the first time. Then the wind pushed her back into the clouds. She looked down to see how high she was, but quickly changed her mind and squeezed her eyes shut in horror. After 15 minutes she realised that she was no longer climbing. She was about 5000 metres and sinking. Her first thought was that she had to try and spiral down.

The amazing descent

She could see the Earth below: 'I could see the Earth coming … wow, like Apollo 13 … I can see the Earth,' she recalled, feeling something like an astronaut humbly, yet triumphantly, returning from the moon.

It was now over three hours since take-off. Ice began to fall off the lines of her glider and the afternoon sun began to warm her face. She had to find somewhere to land. Ewa surveyed the ground stretched out below her but couldn't see a road or anything to indicate where she was. But then she was relieved to see a small farmhouse. She took control, flew towards it and began spiralling down. She managed to land safely.

Once on the ground, she lay exhausted and confused. She wanted to run, but she didn't have the strength. She lay there for several minutes, physically and emotionally unable to call for help. But then, there was a call for her. Her crew had been trying to contact her. Finally, they got through, overjoyed to hear her voice, having tracked her miraculous climb and descent through her global positioning and radio equipment. Ewa had landed 60 kilometres from her launch site.

Ewa was found covered with ice and her body battered with bruises from the hailstones. She had frostbite on her extremities and her ears were nearly frozen off. The fact that she had been unconscious probably saved her life because her heart and body functions slowed down. Doctors treated her for first-second degree frostbite on her ears, first degree frostbite on her face and second-third degree on her legs. Her head was wrapped up in bandages; her ears were so mutilated that she jokingly commented that she looked like ET.

News of her miraculous ascent spread quickly via an online paragliding chatroom; while newspaper headlines of the day revelled in the miraculous nature of her survival: 'Paraglider hailed luckiest woman alive', 'How I rode to the heavens and back', 'Death-defying German paraglider pilot'.

Showing her mental toughness and unfailing love for the sport, Ewa spent only an hour in a hospital for observation and bounced back to compete in the Championships two weeks later. Former world record holder Godfrey Wenness, the organiser of the Championships, summed up the miraculousness of Ewa's ordeal when he said, 'Not even 747s fly through storm cells.'

It seemed impossible, but the impossible happened. And it's an image that stays with you: a free spirit soaring upwards into the heavens, bold, fearless, full of life and full of dreams.

REFERENCES

Abbreviations used:
ABC Australian Broadcasting
Corporation News
ADV The Advertiser
AFP Agence France Presse
AGE The Age
AP Associated Press Newswires
ATSB Australian Transport Safety
Bureau
AU The Australian
BUL The Bulletin
CEN Centralian Advocate
CET Coventry Evening Telegraph
(UK)
CM The Courier Mail
CMEX Cooma-Monaro Express
CT Canberra Times
CP Cairns Post
CWP Cairns Weekend Post
DEX Daily Express (UK)
DMER Mackay Daily Mercury
DML Daily Mail (UK)
DMUK The Daily Mirror (UK)
DP Daily Post (Liverpool UK)
DT The Daily Telegraph
DTM The Daily Telegraph Mirror
DTUK The Daily Telegraph (UK)
GCB The Gold Coast Bulletin
GUA The Guardian (UK)
HA Honolulu Advertiser (US)
HM Hobart Mercury
HS Herald Sun
IM Illawarra Mercury
IND The Independent (UK)
INDS The Independent on Sunday
(UK)
IRE Irish Examiner (Ireland)

KYN Kyodo News (Japan)
MD Manly Daily
MIR The Mirror (UK)
NEW Newsweek
NH Newcastle Herald
NTN/ST Northern Territory News/
Sunday Territorian
NYT New York Times (US)
NZH New Zealand Herald
REU Reuters
SA Sunday Age
SCMP South China Morning Post
SH Sun Herald
SHS Sunday Herald Sun
SM Sunday Mail
SMH The Sydney Morning Herald
SOS Scotland on Sunday
ST Sunday Telegraph
STIM Sunday Times (Perth Australia)
SUN The Sun (UK)
TB Townsville Bulletin
TBI The Bowen Independent
TES The Evening Standard (UK)
TS Times & Star (Cumbria UK)
TT The Times (UK)
WA The West Australian
WM Western Mail (Wales)
WP Washington Post (US)

CHAPTER 1: OCEAN

The Lonergans
AGE 2/02/1998; 6/02/1998;
28/02/1998; 9/03/1998; 25/04/1998;
AUS 29/01/1998; 4/02/1998;
6/02/1998; 7/02/1998; 9/02/1998;
2/07/1998; 17/07/1998
CM 6/02/1998; 24/02/1998;
3/07/1998

DT 30/01/1998; 31/01/1998;
7/02/1998; 21/02/1998; 28/03/1998
HS 31/01/1998; 4/02/1998
IM 30/01/1998; 31/01/1998;
17/02/1998
SHS 1/02/1998; 22/02/1998
SMH 30/01/1998; 31/01/1998;
2/07/1998
ST 1/02/1998; 15/02/1998;
22/02/1998
TT 30/01/1998
WA 9/03/1998
**Ray Boundy/Dennis Murphy/
Lindy Horton**
DM 27/07/1983
SMH 27/07/1983; 28/07/1983;
19/02/1988
Lienne Schellekens
CM 30/12/2002
CP 30/12/2002; 31/12/2002;
1/01/2003; 6/01/2003; 10/01/2003
SMH 30/12/2002
Richard Jordan
AP 31/01/2002; 1/02/2002;
4/02/2002; 2/04/2002
DML 2/02/2002
DTUK 9/02/2002
GUA 16/04/2002
IND 1/02/2002
REU 1/02/2002
SMH 20/04/2002
Robert King
AP 15/04/2002
CM 3/01/2007; 6/01/2007
DT 9/02/2002
GUA 16/04/2002
NYT 21/05/2002
REU 15/04/2002
SMH 16/04/2002; 20/04/2002
Chris Newbrook

DMER 15/12/2006
DMUK 20/12/2006
TB 14/12/2006
WM 16/12/2006
Ursula Clutton
AGE 14/01/2000; 17/01/2000
AUS 14/01/2000; 15/01/2000
CT 13/01/2000
SMH 13/01/2000; 14/01/2000
AM, ABC Radio 12/01/2000
7.30 Report, ABC TV, 13/01/2000
Steve Irwin
AGE 05/09/2006; 6/09/2006
AUS 27/01/2006; 05/09/2006
CM 5/09/2006; 6/09/2006;
DT 5/09/2006; 6/09/2006;
9/09/2006; 30/12/2006
HS 17/01/2006
NEW (US Edition) p64, 15/01/2007
NYT 20/01/2007
SMH 5/09/2006; 6/09/2006
Enough Rope with Andrew Denton:
Episode 30 transcript 6/10/2003
www.abc.net.au/news
Jeff Zahmel
AUS 27/12/2000; 6/09/2006
SMH 6/04/1988

CHAPTER 2: BEACH

Sarah Whiley
ADV 10/01/2006
AGE 9/01/2006; 14/01/2006
AUS 10/01/2006; 16/01/2006
CM 10/01/2006; 11/01/2006
DT 9/01/2006
SM 15/01/2006; 23/07/2006;
24/12/2006
SMH 13/01/2006

www.amazingaustralia.com.au
www.cdnn.info
Raymond Short
DT 28/02/1966
HA 28/02/1966
IM 28/02/1966
www.elasmo-research.org/education/
white_shark
Marcia Hathaway
DM 28/01/1963; 29/01/1963
SMH 29/01/1963; 27/01/2004
Yondon Dungu
SH 4/02/2007
ST 4/02/2007; 11/04/2007
www.news.com.au
Ali Ibrahim and Samir Chakik
AP 22/01/2007
DT 24/01/2007
SMH 24/01/2007

CHAPTER 3: SEASHORE

**Charles Garbutt/'CHG'/
Coneshell**
CP 27/06/1935
The Medical Journal of Australia, 4 April,
1936, pp. 464-466/ H. Flecker
www:grimwade.biochem.unimelb.
edu.au/cone/deathby.html
Commonwealth Electoral Roll
(Queensland) 1922. Queensland
Family History Society Inc 2006.
CD-ROM.Version 1.01.
Bruce East
AGE 24/07/2005
Phillip Cartledge/Jocelyn Jones
DM 31/08/1965
MER 31/08/1965
SMH 30/08/1965

SUN 31/08/1965
Underhill, David. *Australia's Dangerous
Creatures*. (First edition, 4th rev.)
Reader's Digest, Surry Hills 1995
Chinese Ship's Doctor/Pufferfish
AUS 30/05/2007
MIR 30/05/2007
WA 30/05/2007
abcnewsonline 29/05/2007
Kirke Dyson-Holland
NTN 21/09/1954
James Ward
SMH 23/06/1967

Underhill, David. ibid.

CHAPTER 4: SUBURBIA

Bruce Campton
AP 13/10/2006
DT 4/11/2006
HM 14/10/2006
www.bluemts.com.au/reptilepark
www.pacificmagazines.com.au
Gordon Wheatley/Funnel webs
AU 23/11/1998
DT 7/01/1980
SMH 31/03/2006; 1/04/2006
James Cully
SMH 4/01/1980; 7/01/1980

CHAPTER 5: BUSH

David Eason/Fraser Island
CM 3/04/2001; 28/4/2001;
15/04/2003; 16/4/2003; 26/4/2003;
12/05/2001; 18/05/2004;
19/05/2004; 7/12/2004; 11/12/2004;
14/6/2005; 17/6/2005

GUA 28/04/2001; 24/04/2002
SMH 7/05/2001
TES 12/5/2001
www.cultureandrecreation.gov.
au/articles/islands
www.fraserisland.au.com
www.fido.org.au
Clinton Gage
AGE 2/05/2001; 3/05/2001
CM 1/05/2001; 2/05/2001;
3/05/2001; 4/05/2001; 5/05/2001;
22/09/2001; 28/01/2002
DT 1/05/2001; 2/05/2001
www.fido.org.au
**Scarlett Corke/Kasey Rowles/
dingo attacks**
AP 11/11/2004
CM 26/02/1999; 4/04/1998;
7/04/1998; 14/02/1999; 9/04/2001;
1/05/2001; 2/05/2001; 15/07/2002;
16/09/2002; 10/11/2004
CP 31/08/2004
DTUK 11/11/2004
Ricardo Sirutis
ADV 19/05/2005
AUS 19/05/2005; 2/07/2005
CM 11/05/2005; 13/05/2005;
14/05/2005; 17/05/2005;
18/05/2005; 19/05/2005;
20/05/2005; 21/05/2005;
24/05/2005; 26/05/2005; 7/06/2005
DT 13/05/2005; 18/05/2005;
19/05/2005
SM 15/05/2005; 22/05/2005;
14/05/2006
SMH 18/05/2005
ST 22/05/2005
Florian Bayard
ADV 13/06/2005; 14/06/2005
AFP 13/06/2005

AP 12/06/2005; 13/06/2005;
15/06/2005
AUS 13/06/2005; 14/06/2005;
15/06/2005
CM 14/06/2005
CP 16/06/2005
DT 13/06/2005
HM 13/06/2005; 14/06/2005
HS 13/06/2005; 14/06/2005
KYN 13/06/2005
NTS/ST 16/06/2005
SMH 13/06/2005; 14/06/2005
STIM 19/06/2005
WA 13/06/2005; 14/06/2005;
15/06/2005
www.abc.net.au/news/australia/wa/
northwa/200506
abcnewsonline 12/06/2005
Barry Tuite/Cassowaries
CM 3/10/1990
CP 8/07/2006
CWP 1/07/2006
SMH 4/10/1990
Philip McLean
CP 17/07/2002

CHAPTER 6: ROCK

Leopold Krifter
AGE 21/02/2004
MD 24/02/2004
ST 22/02/2004
Warren MacDonald
ADV 10/05/2006
AUS Magazine 14/05/2005
CP 5/05/2006
DT 25/04/2007
TB 20/05/2006

"I Should't Be Alive" Channel Nine,
1 May 2007
MacDonald, Warren. "A Test of Will".
Prahan, Vic: Hardie Grant Books,
2005.

Jeroen van der Zwaan
CP 21/01/2003; 22/01/2003
abcnewsonline 22/01/2003

CHAPTER 7: MOUNTAIN

Stuart Diver/Thredbo Landslide
AGE 9/08/1997; 14/08/1998
AUS 1/08/1997; 2/08/1997
DT 1/08/1997
HS 31/07/1997; 1/08/1997
SA 3/08/1997
SHS 28/05/2006
www.parliament.nsw.gov.au/prod/
parlment/hanstrans
www.lawlink.nsw.gov.au/.../vwfiles/
Thredbo_Final_Report
Zuzana Stevichova
AP 20/12/2003
AUS 22/12/2003
CMEX 23/12/2003
DT 21/12/2003; 22/12/2003
CMEX 23/12/2003
SH 21/12/2003
SMH 20/12/2003
www.worldnewsaustralia.com.au
Snowboarders
AGE 13/08/1999;19/08/1999
AUS 14/08/1999; 21/08/1999
DT 13/08/1999; 14/08/1999;
15/11/1999
MD 28/07/2006
NH 19/11/1999

SMH 3/07/2003; 16/08/1999;
20/08/1999; 17/11/1999
ST 15/08/1999; 31/10/1999;
21/11/1999; 25/06/2000
AM Archive 12/08/1999
7.30 Report 16/11/1999
Outdoor Australia Apr/May 2003
The World Today Archive 17/11/1999

CHAPTER 8: BILLABONG

Isabel von Jordan
AP 1/01/2003; 30/08/2004;
31/08/2004; 2/09/2004
AUS 31/08/2004
CET 24/10/2002
CM 2/09/2004; 4/09/2004
DT 12/01/2005
HM 30/08/2004; 31/08/2004
NTN 24/10/2002
NTN/ST 4/09/2004; 24/10/2004
NZH 2/09/2004
www.nt.gov.au/justice/docs/courts/
coroner/findings/2004/von_jordan.
pdf
www.thesun.co.uk
Ginger Meadows
DT 31/03/1987; 10/04/1987
SMH 3/04/1987
WA 30/05/1987; 30/06/2004
WP 10/04/1987
Newsday 2/04/1987
www.ahs.org.au
www.finetravel.com
www.kimberleysociety.org
www.ontheroad.com.au
Alicia Sorohan
DM (UK) 12/10/2004
SM 28/08/2005

STIM 17/10/2004
www.itsanhonour.gov.au
www.smh.news.com/national/
grandma-returns-to-scene-of-croc-
attack
Brett Mann
AP 29/08/2005
DMUK 24/12/2003
DP 31/12/2003
DT 3/01/2004
NTN/ST 3/01/2004; 7/01/2004;
5/09/2004; 14/12/2004; 21/12/2004;
22/05/2006
SUN (UK) 31/12/2003
TB 29/08/2005
abcnewsonline 5/01/2004

CHAPTER 9: OUTBACK

Gabriele Grossmueller
DT 16/04/2005
IRE 17/12/98
SMH 18/12/1998
www.courts.sa.gov.au/courts/
coroner/findings/findings_2000/
grossmueller.finding
Ethel Hetherington
AGE 29/10/2004
BUL 13/02/2007 Vol. 125; No. 7
DEX 28/10/2004
DML 28/10/2004
GUA 28/10/2004
SMH 27/10/2004; 28/10/2004
TS 5/11/2004; 13/11/2004
TT 29/10/2004
www.abc.net.au/news
www.cumberland-new.co.uk
www.news.bbc.co.uk
www.news.independent.co.uk

www.telegraph.co.uk
www.thesun.co.uk
www.timesandstar.co.uk
Masa Hira Ono
AGE 4/01/1994
DTM 4/01/1994
SMH 31/01/1994; 4/09/1994
WA 4/01/1994
www.abc.net.au/science
Thomas Sykes
AGE 14/12/2003
AUS 13/12/2003
INDS 14/12/2003
SOS 14/12/2003
www. abc.net.au/kimberley/news
www.abc.net.au/news
www.aics.wa.edu.au
www.edinburghnews.scotsman.com
Howard Holdsworth
AGE 13/12/2003
INDS 14/12/2003
www.abc.net.au/news
www.abc.net.au/wa
www.news.bbc.co.uk
www.telegraph.co.uk
Robert Bogucki
AUS 4/09/1999
SCMP 2/09/1999
SMH 19/08/1999: 20/08/1999;
21/08/1999; 24/08/1999
WA 4/09/1999
WA *BigWeekend* 4/09/1999
Azaria Chamberlain
AUS 7/04/1998
CM 14/08/2000
CT 26/07/2005
DT 17/08/2005
GUA 28/07/2001
NTN/ST 6/07/2004

Bryson, John. *Evil Angels: the disappearance of Azaria Chamberlain.* Hodder Headlines, Sydney 2000
www.lindychamberlain.com
David Brett/Falling off Uluru
SH 9/08/1998
SMH 3/02/1986; 5/02/1986; 2/04/1986; 19/04/1986; 10/09/1987; 23/07/1994; 24/02/1997; 9/08/1998; 19/12/1998; 29/12/1998; 29/08/1999; 8/02/2004; 16/03/2006; 30/11/2006
www.ayersrockresort.com.au/geology
www.environment.gov.au/parks/publications/annual/05-06/uluru
www.wayOutback.com.au/uluru-geology
Bryson, John. *Evil Angels: the disappearance of Azaria Chamberlain.* Hodder Headlines, Sydney 2000
Ricketson, Matthew. *Writing Feature Stories.* Allen & Unwin, Crows Nest 2004
www.lindychamberlain.com.au

CHAPTER 10: SKY

Anthony Fraser/Hot air balloon
AGE 15/08/1989
DM 14/08/1989
DT 14/08/1989
SMH 14/08/1989;15/08/1989; 16/08/1989
www.aph.gov.au/Hansard/reps/dailys/dr280696
www.aph.gov.au/Hansard/reps/dailys/dr280897
www.ema.gov.au/ema/emadisasters

Australian Safety Transport Bureau (ATSB), Aircraft Occurrence Report No. 198900820
Benni the Iceman
AGE 8/01/2007
AP 8/01/2007
CP 9/01/2007
GCB 9/01/2007
SMH 9/01/2007
www.blog.central.is/minningumbenna
Ewa Wisnierska/He Zhongpin
AGE 17/02/2007; 1/03/2007
AP 16/02/2007; 20/02/2007
DT 6/03/2007
NZH 17/02/2007
SMH 17/02/2007
ABC transcripts 16/02/2007

ANIMALS

Blue-ringed octopus
www.usq.edu.au
www.barrierreefaustralia.com
Crocodile
AGE 6/11/2004
WA 2/03/2005
www. fairfax.com.au
www.animalplanet.com.au
www.nt.gov.au
Dingo
CM 1/05/2001
SHS 12/04/1998
www.amazingaustralia.com.au/animals/dingo_attacks

General

John A. Williamson ed. (et al). (itals)
Venomous and Poisonous Marine Animals: a Medical and Biological Handbook, UNSW Press, Sydney 1996
Underhill, David. *Australia's Dangerous Creatures* (First edition, 4th rev.) Reader's Digest, Surry Hills 1995

Irukandji/Box jelly fish
AUS 10/01/2006
AUS magazine 28/01/2006
TIM 27/12/1997

Shark
www.amonline.net.au
Sharks: silent hunters of the deep. (First ed 2nd rev.) Reader's Digest, Surry Hills 1990

Snake
AGE 29/12/2005; 1/02/2007
www.australianfauna.com
www.nationalparks.nsw.gov.au
www.reptilepark.com.au
www.zoo.org.au

Spider
www.amonline.net.au

Mateship
www.cultureandrecreation.gov.au/articles/mateship

Scuba diving
www.injuryupdate.com.au

Tourist fatalities
DT 5/02/2007, p. 11, 'Deadly destination: Australia's hidden toll'
www.parliament.nsw.gov.au/prod/parlment/publications.nsf/0/BCE13189D9366B4DCA256ECF000793E0/ tourism in NSW: After September 11 Briefing Paper No. 6/2004 by John Wilkinson (f) Tourist Safety

OTHER

Bush
www.cultureandrecreation.gov.au/articles/bush

Explorers
Lewis, Wendy, Simon Balderstone and John Bowan. *Events that Shaped Australia,* New Holland, Sydney 2006

Lost
www.museum.vic.gov.au/forest/humans/bush.html